ACROSS THE DEEP BLUE SEA

Across the Deep Blue Sea

The Saga of
Early Norwegian Immigrants

Odd S. Lovoll

MINNESOTA
HISTORICAL
SOCIETY PRESS

This project received support from
Institusjonen Fritt Ord / Freedom of Expression Foundation, Oslo, Norway
Norsk faglitterær forfatter og oversetterforening /
Norwegian Non-Fiction Writers and Translators Association, Oslo, Norway
The Ella and Kaare Nygaard Foundation, St. Olaf College, Northfield, Minnesota

www.mnhspress.org
The Minnesota Historical Society Press is a member of the
Association of American University Presses.
Manufactured in the United States of America
10 9 8 7 6 5 4 3 2 1
⊚ The paper used in this publication meets the minimum requirements
of the American National Standard for Information Sciences—
Permanence for Printed Library Materials, ANSI Z39.48–1984.

International Standard Book Number
ISBN: 978-0-87351-961-8 (paper)
ISBN: 978-0-87351-972-4 (e-book)

Library of Congress Cataloging-in-Publication Data
available upon request.

This and other Minnesota Historical Society Press books
are available from popular e-book vendors.

Front cover: top: *Nornen*, Korvette, photo by Anders Beer Wilse, Norwegian
Maritime Museum; bottom: photo by Louis W. Hill, MNHS collections

For Else

Contents

ACROSS THE DEEP BLUE SEA

Introduction

cross the Deep Blue Sea takes a new look at an early chapter in Norwegian emigration history and expands its focus to include historical developments in the Norwegian homeland, the United States, and Canada. From 1850 and for some twenty years, Quebec, Montreal, and other Canadian port cities became the gateway for Norwegian emigrants to North America, replacing New York as the main destination. Norwegian sailing ships engaged in passenger traffic until 1874, after which they lost out in the competition with transatlantic steamships for this financially rewarding transport.

Much of history becomes a record of humanity's struggle for survival and search for happiness; indeed, this might be the theme of any historical work. In a larger context there is as well the desire for national expansion and aggrandizement, demonstrated frequently in commercial enterprise and in the aggressive pursuit of power by individuals and political entities. The Vikings were the first Europeans to set foot on North America around the year 1000, though their explorations did not lead to permanent settlements. The arrival of the French nearly five hundred years later and their claim of possession introduced a persistent European presence and a belligerent occupation and exploitation of resources; the creation of New France, which at the height of its power in the early 1700s covered an immense territory, manifested the force of European conquest. But the colonial powers

3

competed, and Britain won in pitched battles against the French; the conflict resulted in New France in 1763 becoming a British possession.

In the American War of Independence, which began some twelve years later, the thirteen British colonies were the great winners and became the United States. A brief historical account of these early developments provides a deeper understanding of the situation in the 1800s. The nineteenth century is, however, of more immediate significance in the saga of immigration. The events leading up to confederation and the creation of the Dominion of Canada in 1867 were a significant stage in Canada's becoming a transcontinental nation.

At this time, Norwegian immigrants encountered a Canada moving along the path of full independence and prosperity. Norwegians had begun to emigrate to the United States a quarter century earlier. These two movements complemented each other, as almost all arrivals in Quebec joined their compatriots who had settled in the Upper Midwest. With the introduction of free trade, Norwegian sailing ships could engage in the lucrative timber trade from Canada to the British Isles. Some of the Norwegian sailing ships transported immigrants on their way west and timber on their return to Europe. This opportunity created wealth and expanded the size and reach of the Norwegian fleet. Norway became the most important foreign shipping nation in the Canadian timber trade. Although the underdog among its Nordic neighbors, Norway during its history back to the Middle Ages excelled in maritime activities. At mid-century both Norway and Canada experienced economic and greater political independence. In 1814 Norway had broken its long union with Denmark but entered into a dynastic union with Sweden. Norway's advances in its economic and political life powered dissolution of the union.

Both Canada and the United States sought immigrants and engaged in aggressive campaigns through propaganda and emigration agents. The efforts to establish Norwegian colonies in Canada largely failed; only in the 1880s did Norwegians begin settling in Canada's prairie provinces. The emigration from Norway had great regional variations in intensity, but all parts of

Norway were by the mid-1850s affected by the overseas exodus. The states of the Upper Midwest—Wisconsin setting the tone and later joined by Minnesota, Iowa, and others—engaged in persistent recruitment of European emigrants, with Nordic and German groups being the dominant settlers. Land-grant railroad companies played a significant role in the competition for immigrant settlers, and their efforts were supported by colonization agents and other financial interests. People were needed to settle and clear the land, to build the railroads, factories, and towns.

An extraordinary story unfolds in the following pages. At its base is the European expansion into North America. Uniquely, the Norwegian perspective expands the history of emigration to include aspects of the overseas exodus frequently overlooked in historical accounts; it treats the growth of a transportation system of sailing ships, the impact on coastal communities, and the composition and experience of the crew, including crew members who abandoned ship. Emigration is traced regionally, and the emigrants' circumstances associated with the Atlantic crossing and landing in the Province of Quebec are outlined. Campaigns to attract immigrants and settlers are fully covered from different perspectives and add new information and insight to the motivating forces of the transatlantic exodus. The human drama of the emigration is emphasized, as is the individual challenge faced by people who during the sailing ship era sought a better life away from the homeland.

chapter 1

Context and Setting

*T*he phrase *the Canadian gateway* denotes the years from 1850 when Quebec City and other seaports in Quebec Province replaced New York as ports of entry for Norwegian immigrants on sailing ships directly from Norway to North America. In fact, the analogy of a gateway may also apply to the entirety of Canada's history. The driving force behind the dramatic shift was the opportunity for Norwegian sailing ships to engage in the lucrative transport of timber from Canada to ports on the British Isles after free trade replaced the earlier restrictive measures of mercantilism. On their crossing to Canada these ships might transport Norwegian immigrants, though most did not do so, carrying ballast instead. Vessels that transported immigrants secured cargo in both directions. Historian Jacob S. Worm-Müller maintains that much of the days of glory for Norwegian sailing ships derived from the trade with Quebec. These years viewed in a broad historical context represent a unique era in the history of the Norwegian exodus across the Atlantic and one that deserves a comprehensive scholarly treatment.[1]

A Viking Footprint

Canadian historians have identified the Norse explorer Leif Erickson, the son of Erik the Red, as "the first historically named individual in Canadian history." His voyage of discovery, from Greenland to the coast of northeastern

North America, occurred around the year 1000 AD, according to *The Saga of the Greenlanders. The Saga of Erik the Red* has him discovering the historically bewitching Vinland directly after being blown off course on his way from Norway to Greenland. The sagas relate how in about 982 the Norwegian-born Icelander Erik the Red, after being exiled for murder, found the rumored land to the northwest, which became known as Greenland. Erik went back to Iceland, and in 985 he returned to Greenland with a large number of colonists. They founded two settlements near the southwestern-most tip of the island, named the Eastern and the Western settlements.

The sagas tell of two ventures, the first one by Leif's brother Thorvald, who with thirty men got to Vinland, where they stayed for two winters before returning to Greenland. About 1012 a much more ambitious and final effort was made to establish a permanent Norse settlement in America. L'Anse aux Meadows, or an area in its vicinity, on the northern point of Newfoundland, seems likely to have been the site, though its precise location is unknown. It also failed. However, archeological finds give evidence that for several hundred years, until the two Norse Greenland settlements were depopulated—the Western Settlement in the fourteenth and the Eastern Settlement in the fifteenth century—Norse Greenlanders launched hunting and trading voyages across the Davis Strait, returning with furs and timber. In the year 2000, Newfoundlanders celebrated the millennium of the Vikings' arrival.[2]

THE ARRIVAL OF THE EUROPEANS

Following this brief encounter with the Norse, the coming of the Europeans eventually resulted in a convergence, perhaps initially a collision, of two worlds. Nearly five hundred years passed after the Viking landing before Europe again explored the New World, beginning with the "discovery" by Christopher Columbus in 1492.

A few years later, in 1497, John Cabot, born like Columbus in the Italian seaport city of Genoa, made it to Newfoundland, followed later by other explorers. "The history of Quebec," to quote from *A People's History of Quebec,* "began formally on Friday July 24, 1534." The reference is to ship captain Jacques Cartier, who on that date sent his seamen ashore at Gaspé Bay, though the exact location has never been determined. Cartier and his men encountered a party of St. Lawrence Iroquois who served as their hosts. The purpose of the landing was "to erect a cross bearing an escutcheon with three fleurs-de-lis and a plate where it was engraved 'Vive le roi de France.'" The ceremony formally claimed possession of the land on behalf of King Francis I. Cartier dubbed it New France.

On a second voyage, in 1535–36, Cartier sailed as far as the village of Stadacona, later the site of Quebec; Cartier also sailed upriver to the Iroquoian village of Hochelaga, at the foot of "Mont Royal," a name Cartier gave the large mountain in the middle of the island of Montreal; the name stuck, and a French settlement eventually rose there. The territory was claimed as a royal French possession—in fact, a second claim to possession of the land. Cartier made a fourth voyage in 1541–42 and again visited Montreal, sailing as far as the Lachine Rapids allowed.

Stadacona, or Quebec, if you will, was the heart of a region known as the "Kingdom of Canada." The name *Canada* is of Iroquoian origin, meaning a village or group of houses; *Iroquoian* refers to the Native people in the St. Lawrence–Great Lakes region. The French hoped to settle the St. Lawrence Valley.[3]

OLD QUEBEC AND NEW FRANCE

The historical account in *Old Quebec: The Fortress of New France* maintains that "the name of [Samuel] Champlain must stand before all others in the history of Quebec." Samuel de Champlain is credited with founding the city of Quebec in 1608, making it, according to the same source, the oldest city in the Western Hemisphere. Champlain was accorded the title of "the father of New France" or "La Nouvelle France," but it took time for the city he founded to grow; it initially served as little more than a fur trading post. However, he came to see it as the hub of a major French settlement in America, and in 1663 New France became a royal French colony.

Cross erected in Gaspé Harbor in 1934 to commemorate the anniversary of the landing of Jacques Cartier in July 1534. *Photo by Odd S. Lovoll*

"For at least the first hundred years of its existence, Quebec was New France; and the story of Quebec in that period is the story of all Canada," the historians Gilbert Parker and Claude Bryan hold. Quebec City became the capital of New France. At its height in 1712, the territory of New France, including the administrative district known as French Louisiana, extended from Newfoundland to the Rocky Mountains and from Hudson Bay to the Gulf of Mexico. Quebec was chosen for its geographic location.

As a fur trading post, Quebec City had the advantage of being close to several indigenous nations; its safe harbor ensured that it could easily be provisioned by transatlantic shipping. It was the deep-sea terminal linking the hinterland with the high seas and the obvious landing point for military reinforcement. Military activities were a part of Quebec City since its founding; consequently, it became a fortified city. Historian André Charbonneau explains the advantages of the site of "Quebec City with its natural defences— its steep promontory, narrow harbour entrance and climate that restricted enemy movements for months on end." He further states, "It became the symbol of the battle between two empires, French and English, on the North American continent."[4]

In the 150 years New France existed, 1608–1760, about ten thousand immigrants came to the colony. Historian Robert Bothwell defines them as follows: "Almost all were French, direct from France; and almost all . . . were Catholic." He continues, "They were not, most of them, a hardy race of peasants of Norman stock." They came from the western provinces of France, a substantial number from Paris and some from other cities. Some came by compulsion, via the army or as punishment for minor infractions. Indentured servants formed another group of settlers. Bothwell quotes two geographers, Cole Harris and John Warkentin, who observed that "most [immigrants] came to Canada because they were sent."

"New France was more than the valley of the St. Lawrence," historian Bothwell observes. Fisheries had brought the French to North America. They fished in the waters off Newfoundland and went up the St. Lawrence River, where they harvested fish and fur. Immigration of Anglo-Normans to eastern Canada from the English Channel islands of Jersey, Guernsey, Sark, and Alderney, located between the Brittany and Cherbourg peninsulas, added an identifiable population to the eastern coastal regions. According to oral history, "Jersey Islanders were among the first seafarers and fishermen to discover the rich fisheries off the Gulf of St. Lawrence." Whether the oral account can be verified or not, Anglo-Normans came from early on to the fishing banks of Newfoundland. They were the third-largest group of Newfoundland pioneers. As descendants of the Normans who ruled England following William the Conqueror in 1066, Anglo-Normans in Canada may hold a special interest for the present study, not simply due to the Norman legacy but even more because of the Jersey dominance in the cod fishery on Quebec's Atlantic coast from the mid-1700s until the 1880s.

New France formed alliances with some Native tribes who joined the French in warfare with the tribes of the Iroquois Confederacy. There was in addition to the conflict with Indian tribes a constant threat and also invasions from the New England colonies; wars between European powers affected the French colony as well. In 1710 the New England colonists besieged Port Royal on the east side of the Bay of Fundy and received the surrender of its garrison. In the Treaty of Utrecht in 1713, Acadia was ceded to Great Britain and became a British colony. Acadia was a distinct colony of New France; Acadians spoke "Acadian French." Then, during the years 1755–62, British colonial officers and New England legislators and militia carried out what is known as the "Great Expulsion." Some 11,500 Acadians were deported from the maritime region, perhaps a case of ethnic cleansing.[5]

The Treaty of Utrecht in 1713 amputated a large portion of New France's territory, not only Acadia—now Nova Scotia—but also Newfoundland. It was a harbinger of the English conquest of New France. Thereafter a period of peace, lasting until 1744, became a time of prosperity. It was New France's "Golden Age." The war that broke out between Britain and France and their respective colonies that year lasted until 1748 and did not resolve any territorial disputes.

Lingering hostility and pitched battles between France and Britain resulted in declarations of war in 1756, the start of the so-called Seven Years' War.

For the inhabitants of New France, now Quebec, it is known as the *Guerre de la Conquête*, or "War of Conquest." It was fought both in Europe and in its colonies around the world. British troops and naval forces were directed to the conquest of New France, engaging in a lengthy military campaign. The fortress of Louisbourg on Île Royale, designed to protect the St. Lawrence entrance, fell to British forces in July 1758. In historian Margaret Conrad's words, "the heart of New France now lay exposed." The campaign against Quebec City culminated in the defeat of the French defenders on the Plains of Abraham—now a memorial park—after a brief battle on September 13, 1759, and formal surrender a few days later. In his journal of the campaign, Captain John Knox of the English fleet described Quebec City: "The City of Quebec consists of two towns, distinguished by the high and low town: they are separated from each other by a steep cliff of rock which is a natural fortification to near two thirds of the upper town, at the same time that it serves as a shelter to the low town from the keen penetrating north-west winds ... The principal strength of Quebec consists of its eminent situation: ship-guns cannot have sufficient elevation to do it any considerable damage."

The following year, British forces converged on Montreal, where Pierre de Rigaud de Vaudreuil, the colony's first Canadian-born governor, surrendered on September 8, 1760. The Treaty of Paris, signed on February 10, 1763, recognized British authority in New France; it was named the Province of Quebec by the English. French Louisiana had not been a theater of war; it was divided along the Mississippi River, with Britain acquiring the eastern section. France ceded the area west of the Mississippi to its ally Spain. "His Britannic Majesty," as stated in the treaty, gave orders "that his new Roman Catholic subjects may profess their religion according to the rites of the Romish church, as far as the laws of Great Britain permit." The Quebec Act of 1774 as passed by the British parliament specifically granted the freedom to profess the Catholic faith. It was, according to historian Peter Moogh, remarkably liberal given the strong religious prejudices of the day. "Catholic emancipation from legal disabilities," Moogh states, "occurred in Canada fifty-five years before it was granted in Great Britain." The 90 percent of the population who in 1790 were Catholic enjoyed greater freedom in Canada than did residents of the same faith in Britain. It was, however, a new era. As historian Conrad states, "The Seven-Year War marked the end of the French Empire in continental North America."[6]

THE AMERICAN WAR OF INDEPENDENCE

Rumblings against English rule in the British colonial empire to the south turned into an armed conflict following a hostile encounter between British troops and colonial militiamen in Lexington and Concord in April 1775. Britain's thirteen North American colonies engaged in a full-scale war for their independence from the British colonial powers the following year. The Declaration of Independence adopted by the Continental Congress on July 4, 1776, announced that the colonies were at war with Britain and regarded themselves as independent states, no longer a part of the British Empire. France entered the war on the rebels' side. The British surrender at York-town, Virginia, on October 17, 1781, secured independence, though the war did not formally end until the articles of peace were signed in 1783. The United States of America was the great winner, but many people in the newly formed country wished to remain British subjects. They became known as Loyalists. Some forty thousand Loyalists emigrated, mainly to Nova Scotia and the colony created in 1784 called New Brunswick, as well as to the region that in 1791 became Upper Canada.

In 1791, then, the name *province* disappeared and was replaced by two names, *Lower Canada* and *Upper Canada*, in reference to their location on the St. Lawrence River, each colony getting an elected assembly and a governor. Greater democracy was, however, constrained by a legislative council's veto. The majority in Lower Canada had French as their mother tongue, and Upper Canada was English speaking; it came into being, as had New Brunswick earlier, to quote Bothwell, "largely in response to Loyalists demands for an accountable local authority equipped with familiar and compatible institutions." Loyalists in other words demanded a separate district where they would feel at home. The status of the French language, which remained strongly positive, was also an issue for the Loyalists before the province was divided. Agitation to assimilate Lower Canada and make it English speaking created tensions between the two groups. At the time, only French-speaking subjects were referred to as "Canadians"; it took several decades before English-speaking people would be called Canadians; only then would the original French-speaking Canadians begin to be known as "French Canadians."[7]

Immigration from the British Isles was promoted, and Canadian authorities offered various land-grant programs, including, in Upper Canada in the early years, efforts "to induce responsible individuals to undertake the settlement of whole townships." Small grants were also made to individuals; the process of distributing lands was gradually remodeled and improved, the goal being to attract as many responsible settlers as possible. Many land companies operated in New Brunswick and Upper Canada alongside colonization agents; it was fertile land, accessible by water and increasingly by road. British immigrants as a rule preferred to go on to Upper Canada. Lower Canada was little favored. There was as well a steady immigration from the United States. The population of Upper Canada grew from twenty thousand in 1792 to an estimated seventy thousand in 1806, reflecting a large movement from south of the border. In 1792 the much more populous Lower Canada numbered 156,000 residents; no more than an estimated ten thousand were English speaking. Nevertheless, Lower Canada had many Anglophone enclaves; Montreal, for example, for much of the nineteenth century was mainly an English-speaking city. It became the distribution, commercial, and financial center for the St. Lawrence basin; the economy of Lower Canada prospered, and Upper Canada grew in wealth and population.[8]

THE DECADES AFTER THE WAR OF 1812

The war between Great Britain and the United States in 1812, with military attacks on Upper Canada, was of course a disruptive, belligerent event. But British North America appeared both externally and internally stable following the war. The colonies had weathered the battles. Emigration from the

British Isles to British North America increased rapidly, with new settlers attracted by economic growth. The timber and lumber that flowed to the British Isles was one factor in bringing development to New Brunswick and the Canadas.

Statistics give evidence of rapid growth. During the 1820s and 1830s, the population in the two Canadas virtually exploded. By 1842 Upper Canada—after the 1840 Act of Union, more correctly Canada West—had a total population of 487,053. Of this, 50.8 percent were Canadian-born English Canadians—a figure that encompasses Canadian-born residents of Irish-, Welsh-, Scottish-, and English-born parentage—and 2.9 percent were Canadian-born French Canadians; 16.1 percent were born in Ireland, 8.4 percent in England and Wales, and 8.1 percent in Scotland; 6.7 percent were born in the United States. If those born in Canada of American parentage are included, the estimate rises to 11.6 percent. An indigenous population of approximately 219,700 may be added to these figures. Lower Canada, now Canada East, had about 670,000 people; the French-Canadian majority held its own as a proportion of the population and grew in numbers. In the course of the second half of the 1850s, however, Canada West surpassed Canada East in population.

Historian Bothwell maintains that "Politics in Lower Canada had always had a racial or linguistic tinge, and the rebellions of 1837–38, though not entirely fought along linguistic lines, nevertheless appealed to the French majority in the province." The political realities of the 1840s reversed the stated hopes for linguistic uniformity sought by anglicizing French Canadians. French-Canadian culture was not submerged; reformers in English and French Canada in the united parliament opposed the old ruling elite and its objectives. A separate and distinct French education system was created, counteracting all expenditures to anglicize French Canadians.

The Act of Union of 1840, proclaimed in February 1841, reunited Upper Canada and Lower Canada, which thereafter became regions rather than provinces, as described above, within the Province of Canada. Montreal was the home of the parliament of Canada from 1844 to 1849, when it was torched by protesters against the adoption of the Rebellion Losses Bill,

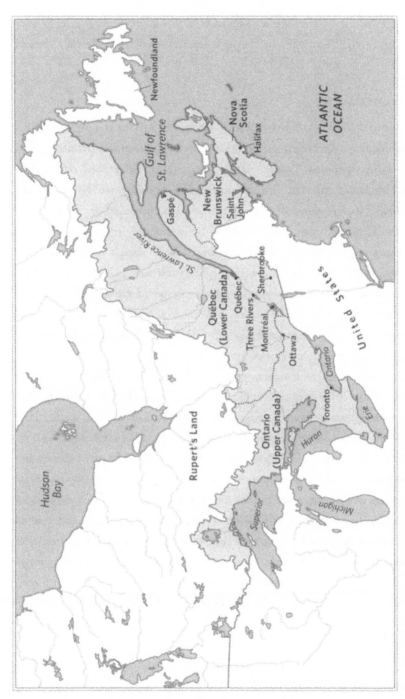

The Dominion of Canada, 1867. *Drawn by Matt Kania*

devised to compensate victims of repression during the rebellions of 1837–38.
The fire ended Montreal's brief stint as the country's capital. In 1857 Ottawa
became the center of state.[9]

CONFEDERATION

Creation of the United Province of Canada may be seen as a prelude to full
confederation. According to Margaret Conrad, the union's architects preferred the cognomen "confederation" rather than "federation," referring to
the American Civil War, "on the unfounded grounds that the latter term
implied a looser structure such as the one that prevailed in the now discredited United States." The feasibility of uniting the colonies, each being
autonomous, had long been considered by British officials and colonial pol-
iticians. In the 1860s, the time seemed ripe to take action. Following deliber-
ations, which did not always run smoothly, the confederation gained support.
This new status took effect on July 1, 1867, after the British North America
Act creating the Dominion of Canada had passed through the British parliament on March 29 of that year.

The Dominion of Canada consisted of the four colonies New Brunswick, Nova Scotia, Upper Canada (Canada West), which became Ontario,
and Lower Canada (Canada East), which retrieved its original name, Quebec—the united provinces were thus again divided. The confederation consequently gave French Canadians a place of their own. The new constitution
established a federal government and provincial governments. Grandiose
buildings were being erected in the new Canadian capital of Ottawa in time
to receive the new Canadian parliament. The Dominion of Canada occupied
of course only a small portion of British North America. Nevertheless, as
historian Desmond Morton states, "The history of Canada as a single
transcontinental nation begins from that date [July 1, 1867]," but, he concludes, "its communities harboured much older history."[10]

THE STORY OF THE SLOOPERS

The rise of mass emigration occurred in the decades between 1815 and 1860.
It was, to quote historian Maldwyn Allen Jones, "one of the wonders of the

age." Nineteenth-century Norwegian group immigration to North America had a colorful beginning with the sailing of the sloop *Restauration* from Stavanger, a town on the southwestern coast of Norway, on July 4, 1825, arriving in New York on October 9 after a dramatic, lengthy journey by way of Madeira. The *Restauration*'s voyage illuminated the spread of the emigration phenomenon; the sailing of the small sloop foreshadowed a mass movement of Norwegians to North America.

Individuals had made it across the Atlantic in previous decades and centuries, as historian Theodore Blegen describes: "There was a not unimportant roundabout filtering of individuals—many of them sailors—from Norway to America in the seventeenth and eighteenth centuries." These were individuals, generally seamen, not associated with the seventeenth-century Scandinavian migration to New Netherland, yet they may be viewed as a continuation of the earlier movement. One finds the Norwegian sailor Cornelius Wilson from Arendal, Norway, on His Majesty's Ship *Raisonable* in the War of Independence; he died in Halifax in 1778 after his service in the Royal British Navy. In 1808 there was Fredrick Peterson, who served as a private at the first Fort Dearborn on the south bank of the Chicago River and was in 1812 killed in battle against a native tribe. Both had likely crossed on a Dutch ship.[11]

Blegen nevertheless makes the obvious point that "Norwegian immigration as a related movement is practically confined to the period since about 1825." Religious considerations motivated the Sloopers, the pioneer emigrants who got their name from the type of ship on which they crossed; they sought a place where they could freely and without restrictions worship God. The desire to seek refuge from religious intolerance was in the Norwegian context a unique aspect of this exodus. Surely the Sloopers also hoped for a better material outcome on the other side of the Atlantic. Actually, economic motives played an important part since prospects at home at the time were not encouraging.

The Sloopers were Quakers and Quaker sympathizers or Haugeans, followers of the great lay Lutheran preacher and revivalist Hans Nielsen Hauge, who led his flock in a pietistic protest against the prevailing rationalism of the Lutheran clergy. He was imprisoned from 1804 to 1814 for his breach of the Conventicle Act, which until it was repealed in 1842 prohibited lay preaching and religious gatherings outside the control of the ordained Lutheran clergy. Both Quakers and Haugeans experienced conflict with officials of state and church; persecution by the clergy of the monopolistic Lutheran state church brought them together. Until religious liberty was granted in the 1840s, dissent and separatism were dealt with harshly; Hauge's imprisonment is a case in point.

Quakerism had been brought to Norway by mariners taken prisoner in the war of 1807 and held in England until the Treaty of Kiel in 1814. While imprisoned, they had repeatedly been visited by Quakers, who had shown much interest in their welfare. George Richardson relates in his 1849 book, *Rise and Progress of the Society of Friends in Norway*, that Enoch Jacobson, a young man from Stavanger and a prisoner on board a boat in the Chatham River, was "by the Spirit of Truth awakened" and became the first Norwegian convert to the teachings of the Society of Friends. He was joined by a small group of Danes and Norwegians—about thirty, according to contemporary reports—who also converted to the beliefs of the Friends. Among these was Lars Larsen (Geilane), the leader of the Sloopers and in reality the only registered member of the Quaker society making the crossing. The Society of Friends was established in Stavanger and Christiania (Oslo). Richardson describes in detail the Friends' missionary activity. Elias Tastad, one of the four imprisoned converts from Stavanger, became the leader of the Quakers in that city; the other three were Lars Larsen (Geilane), Ole Franck, and Even Samuelsen. Tastad described how the society was formed: "On our return, we were as poor and strange servants; yet we came to live so near one another, that we kept up our meetings for worship, two or three times in the week, constantly; when a few others sometimes came and sat with us, either in a loft or a chamber."

Tastad also explains the trials and afflictions they endured as "a strange and despised people"; their sufferings, Tastad wrote, "were principally caused by the clergy, who stirred up the magistrates to persecution." The Stavanger

Society of Friends had only eight members when founded on August 29, 1818, in the home of Lars Larsen (Geilane). The Friends nevertheless had considerable influence. In his study of ecclesiastical reform, Andreas Seierstad supports Richardson's contention that it was "the little body of Friends in Norway" that through its strong faith, patience, and suffering made the Norwegian dissenter law of 1845 more tolerant and liberal than it otherwise might have been. The law protected the free public exercise of religion for non-Lutheran Christian congregations.

The international character of the Society of Friends, whose members were connected with fellow believers in many parts of the world, gave them knowledge about existing conditions and opportunities in America. Norwegian Quakers had lively contact with English Quakers. After the Sloopers, the Stavanger Quakers continued to play a role in Norwegian emigration. In the 1850s and '60s, they became involved in the colonization of Quebec.[12]

The *Restauration* was only thirty-nine tons, fifty-five feet long, and sixteen feet wide. It was built as a single-masted sailing ship, in Hardanger in 1801, and named *Emanuel;* later it was rebuilt as a sloop, also with a single mast but with a different rigging, and renamed *Restauration.* The Sloopers purchased the ship themselves, which highlights the challenges faced by those who desired to cross the Atlantic: no regular communications existed between Norwegian ports and any port in America. The Sloopers numbered fifty-two passengers and crew, all intending to settle in America. In the course of the voyage Lars Larsen's wife Martha gave birth to a girl who was baptized Margaret Allen after a well-known English Quaker. Most of the passengers hailed from the rural parish of Tysvær, north of the city of Stavanger, and a few from the city itself.

When landing in New York, the Sloopers were welcomed by Cleng Peerson—an enigmatic actor in the drama of the pioneer emigration—together with a group of Quakers. Peerson's historical significance has accorded him the title "the father of Norwegian immigration," though some historians have claimed that his general importance has been exaggerated. In any case, he clearly served as the advance agent of the immigrants of 1825, and there can be no doubt about his significant role in the early emigration. In the summer of 1821, together with Knud Olsen Eide, who died not long after arriving in America, Peerson journeyed from Stavanger to New York by way of Gothenburg, Sweden. This route became common for Norwegian emigrants between 1825 and 1850; in Gothenburg travelers found passage on Swedish sailing ships carrying cargoes of iron for American ports.

Peerson remained in the United States until 1824, when he made a brief trip to Norway to report on his findings. Encouraged by his optimism, the group in the Stavanger district made preparations to emigrate. After his return to America with traveling companion Andrew Stangeland, he was engaged in preparing for their arrival. Peerson purchased land in western and northern New York State on the shores of Lake Ontario in Kendall township. With the assistance of American Quakers, most of the Sloopers moved to this township; there they struggled through the hardships of pioneer life. Kendall was the first Norwegian settlement in the United States.[13]

EMIGRANT TRAFFIC

Emigrant traffic was the backbone of the transatlantic trade. The transportation of millions of emigrants from Europe beginning in the 1820s and growing dramatically throughout the century resulted in the establishment of large passenger shipping firms in England, the United States, and the German ports of Bremen and Hamburg. With regular sailings, the growing number of emigrants provided shipowners in many countries with possibilities for undreamed-of profits. The same story, though on a much smaller scale, is found in Norway as well: emigration to the United States played a considerable role in the development of Norwegian shipping, providing an opportunity to find new overseas markets and promoting the formation of independent shipping firms.

There is no record of a group emigration from Norway between 1825 and 1836, though individuals made their way to America during these years. Gjert G. Hovland, who came to Kendall in 1831, was one of the early arrivals. Knud

Langeland, an emigrant in 1843 and later prominent in Norwegian American journalism, describes Hovland as "an enlightened and liberal farmer from Hardanger in Bergen Diocese." Hovland's letters sent back to Norway were a major factor in the dissemination of information about the United States in his home diocese of Bergen; hundreds of copies of Hovland's letters were in circulation, and from 1835 to 1843 many were even published in local and regional newspapers. They awakened great interest in America and made people decide to emigrate.

The westward movement of the Kendall settlers was a significant development in the history of Norwegian immigration. The Erie Canal, an engineering marvel completed in 1825, linked the waters of Lake Erie in the west to the Hudson River in the east; it was the route taken by the Sloopers that

The full-rigged *Hebe*, built in 1856 at the shipyard Georgenes in Bergen, is generally considered to be the masterpiece of the shipwright Annanias Dekke. In 1856 it made its first crossing from Bergen to Quebec in the record time of four weeks. *Stavanger maritime museum, Stavanger, Norway*

same year. The canal opened up to settlement enormous land areas in the upper Mississippi basin. Cleng Peerson again became a trailblazer. In 1833 he traveled west in search of lands suitable for Norwegian settlement. It was a truly epic journey as Peerson walked from western New York to Ohio, across southern Michigan, through northern Indiana, to Illinois and the small collection of log cabins that was Chicago.

Peerson made many excursions to inspect the land. He discovered what became the Promised Land, the land of milk and honey, in the Fox River Valley in La Salle County, Illinois, about seventy miles southwest of Chicago. The Fox River community became the second Norwegian settlement in America and the first in the Midwest. The year 1834 marked the beginning of migration from Kendall to the new colony in the West. And during 1834 and 1835 most of the Kendall settlers moved to their new Fox River Valley home. In April 1835 Gjert Hovland announced in a letter to a friend that "We now intend to move farther inland where you can make better bargains in buying fertile land and where it is easier to start." And in an 1838 letter he described it as "Canaan . . . when we consider the fertile soil that without manuring brings forth such rich crops of everything." He continued, "Norway cannot be compared to America any more than a desert can be compared to a garden in full bloom."[14]

EMIGRATION AND THE WESTWARD MOVEMENT

Only after a permanent settlement in the Midwest stood ready to welcome new immigrants from Norway did annual emigration commence. The Fox River community became an important receiving station as well as a dispersal point to new settlements. It functioned as a mother colony. In addition to "America letters"—correspondence like Hovland's from immigrants to kin and friends back home—people in Norway received firsthand information about the prospects for success as settlers in the Mississippi River Valley when Knud Anderson Slogvig, an immigrant of 1831, paid a visit to Norway in 1835. He had moved from Kendall to the Fox River settlement the year before. In 1836 the Stavanger shipping firm J. A. Køhler & Co. took up the transportation of emigrants as a distinctive commerce. That year two Norwegian sailing vessels, the brigs *Den norske Klippe* and *Norden*, crossed over from Stavanger to New York.

Slogvig served as guide for the emigrants on the *Norden*. The two ships combined had 167 passengers, all headed for the Fox River settlement. Bjørn Andersen Kvelve from Vikedal was one of the passengers on the *Norden;* he was at odds with officialdom, like many of the early emigrants; he had connections with the Quakers in Stavanger and was influenced by Elias Tastad in his decision to emigrate. Slogvig was himself a Quaker, and also on board was Martha Trulsdatter, one of the Stavanger society's founders. As Blegen writes, "In addition there were emigrants who made it to New York via Gothenburg." A total of about two hundred Norwegians emigrated in this first year of annual departures. Most proceeded to the Fox River settlement in La Salle County; a few remained in Chicago and formed the nucleus of what would become a large Norwegian urban colony.

Two more emigrant ships, the brig *Enigheden* from Stavanger and the bark *Ægir* from Bergen, departed the following year. The *Ægir* has special historical interest because it predates the practice of transforming vessels from carrying freight to transporting passengers, as was common in the later traffic to Quebec. It left Bergen on April 7 under Captain Christian K. Behrens with eighty-four passengers, mainly from present-day Hordaland *fylke* (province). Behrens had made a voyage to New York with freight the year before and there gained knowledge about emigrant ships. After his return to Norway, he remodeled his vessel for passenger service, intending to accommodate the considerable number of Norwegians who were planning to emigrate. Some had even sold their farms.

The most notable passenger on the *Ægir* in 1837 was Ole Rynning, a pastor's son from Snåsa. Through his leadership and his guidebook, *True Account of America for the Information and Help of Peasant and Commoner,* his "influence on the early Norwegian emigration was as great as that of Cleng Peerson and

possibly greater," according to Blegen. His fatal decision, influenced by speculators, to skip the Fox River community and form a small settlement in
a marshy area south of Chicago known as Beaver Creek had tragic consequences. Most of the settlers, including Rynning, perished from malaria during the first two years, and the few survivors fled to the Fox River.

The Fox River settlement in La Salle County expanded and branched
out south and north. In 1847 a Norwegian settlement was established in Lee
County to the north. Gary Krahenbuhl gives a captivating account of his
great-grandparents Elias Espe and Guri Bly (Bleie) and their experience as
emigrants. They both grew up on farms in the Hardanger district of Norway.
In 1857, Elias, then twenty-three years old, and his one-year-older brother
Peter crossed over to Quebec City from Bergen on the small schooner *Jørgen
Brunchorst*, and from there traveled to Chicago by train and then south to the
Norwegian settlement in Lee County.

The economic downturn the year they arrived made for poor wages.
Showing the resourcefulness and venturesome spirit of pioneer settlers, the
two brothers along with other young men caught gold fever and headed west
in the spring of 1859. They worked on their own prospecting in California
until 1864, when they returned to Illinois, each with the considerable amount
of $6,000 in gold. Krahenbuhl provides a colorful depiction of their jour-
ney west and back.

The following year they brought their parents over to Lee County, where
they resided for the rest of their lives. This act—not overly common—
illustrates the accommodations that many immigrants made. Around 1870,
Elias and Peter bought farmland in eastern Lee County; the land has remained in the family since. The church edifice completed in 1874 and built
on land donated by Elias Espe became, as in most rural Norwegian settlements, the central point of the community. Local loyalty to Hardanger
defined the settlement.

Great-grandmother Guri Bly arrived in the port of Quebec on the bark
Immanuel in the summer of 1872 at the age of twenty-five. She suffered great
seasickness during the many weeks of the voyage and reportedly said, "If I

Sandfærdig Beretning

om

Amerika,

til Oplysning og Nytte for Bonde og Menigmand.

Forfattet af

En Norsk, som kom derover i Juni Maaned 1837.

Christiania.

—

1838.

Title page of Ole Rynning's guide *True Account of America. Credit: the Norwegian-American Historical Association, Northfield, MN*

ever reach the shore, I'll never go back to Norway." Family lore does not record how she met Elias, but on July 30, 1876, they were married. Elias Espe was then a widower with two children from his first marriage. Together they had six children. True to her word, Guri never traveled on a boat again and never saw the members of her family who remained in Norway. Most emigrants during the era of sailing ships experienced this same estrangement from the homeland.[15]

The year 1837 is notable in the spread of "America fever" (*Amerikafeber*), as it was called, to eastern Norway. Brothers Ole Knudsen Nattestad and Ansten Knudsen Nattestad from Veggli, Rollag parish in Numedal, are central actors in the pioneer exodus from their part of the country. Dissemination of information about America and opportunities there is a major factor in explaining the exodus from different regions of Norway. The Nattestads related how they learned about America when they went to the west coast to buy sheep, which they hoped to sell at a profit. "While roaming around Stavanger," Ole Nattestad explains, "we heard much talk about a land called America." And, as Ole relates, "It was the first time we had ever heard the name." The idea of emigrating took form and "matured into firm determination."

In the book *Beskrivelse over en Reise til Nordamerica* (Description of a Journey to North America), published in 1839, a rare early document, Ole Nattestad gives a full account of his and Ansten's departure from Gothenburg on May 11, 1837, on the ship *Hilda*, a large vessel with a cargo of iron. It made the crossing to Fall River, Rhode Island, in only thirty-two days. From there the brothers made their way inland via New York, Albany, and the Great Lakes. In Detroit they met Ole Rynning and his party. They got passage to Chicago and from there on Rynning's advice accompanied him to Beaver Creek. The following spring, before the swamp fever, or malaria, broke out and the homestead was abandoned, Ansten Nattestad returned to Norway, as he relates, to inform people "of the great difference in opportunities for laboring people here and in Norway, especially for the farmer." Ole Nattestad for his part went to the Fox River settlement and then explored farming land across the Illinois-Wisconsin line. There he founded the Norwegian settlement at Jefferson Prairie in Rock County, Wisconsin.

When about sixty years old in 1869, Ole Nattestad reminisced in an interview with Svein Nilsson, editor of *Billed-Magazin*, about his life as an immigrant and pioneering settler:

> In the spring of 1838 my brother Ansten took a trip to Norway while I worked as a day laborer in northern Illinois. On July 1, 1838, I arrived at the place where I now live, near the center of Clinton township in Rock County, Wisconsin. Here I bought land and was thus the first Norwegian to settle in this state. Neither, to the best of my knowledge, had any Norwegian previously set foot on Wisconsin soil nor entered the state to inspect land. For a whole year I did not see any countryman of mine but lived secluded, without friends, family or companions.

Ansten Nattestad returned the spring of 1839 with a large group of people, mainly from Numedal and Upper Telemark. The group had sailed from Drammen on the ship *Emilia* directly to New York, some by way of Gothenburg, which was the route most immigrants took in 1839. Ansten's own account, printed in *Billed-Magazin* in 1869, described the group's dispersal after arriving in Chicago:

> In Chicago I learned that while I was in Norway my brother Ole had settled in Wisconsin. Some members of our party went to the Fox River settlement where they had friends, while several single persons got work in or near Chicago. The rest—that is to say most of them—went up north with me. Among them were a few who settled in Rock Run township, Stephenson County [Illinois], about thirty miles west of Jefferson Prairie, and became the founders of a Norwegian settlement in that part of the state. Others of my party went to Rock Prairie (Luther Valley), a few miles west of my brother's place. In the fall of 1839 the rest of the group and I came to Jefferson Prairie, where we bought land and began the toilsome pioneer life.[16]

The Decade of the 1840s

Norwegian statistics for the last five years of the 1830s show that about twelve hundred Norwegians emigrated; these figures differ from the American statistics. Blegen, however, maintains that the round Norwegian numbers are approximately correct. For the decade of the 1840s, he agrees, the emigration from Norway to America totaled seventeen thousand. Blegen's summary reads, "The story of Norwegian immigration from 1837 to the middle of the century is one of increasing volume and of steady expansion in settlement from the Illinois nucleus to the West, Northwest, and Southwest."

Wisconsin would become the most important destination for Norwegian immigrants landing in Quebec beginning in the 1850s; *Lyna*, the first sailing ship carrying passengers, arrived late in the summer of 1850. The state government engaged heavily in encouraging new arrivals to settle in the Badger

The small vessel *Skjoldmøen* left on its hazardous America voyage from Bergen on April 12, 1863, and docked in Chicago on June 16. Direct sailing to Chicago from Norway had begun the previous year with the voyage of the brig *Sleipner. Stiftelsen Bergens sjøfartsmuseum, Bergen, Norway*

State. It is consequently important to give an overview of Norwegian settlements in Illinois and Wisconsin before 1850. These pioneer communities became important magnets for Norwegian immigrants in the following decades, even though some Norwegians did indeed remain in Canada.

Most immigrants after 1836 crossed the Atlantic on Norwegian brigs and barks. Historian Carlton Qualey terms emigration in the period up to 1850 as "small beginnings." A rapid increase came after that time. In the 1840s, some immigrants continued to leave for America via Gothenburg on Swedish and American ships that transported iron. Le Havre, France, became a center for European emigrant traffic in these years, and some Norwegians chose this route. Almost all immigrants toward the end of the 1840s landed in New York.

"The bulk of the Norwegian immigrants," as Blegen writes, "were streaming into Wisconsin in the 1840s." The 1850 federal census shows that there were 8,651 Norwegian residents in the state that year. The pioneer communities became both receiving stations and points of departure for new settlements in the state. In Dane County, a circle of Norwegian settlements was established around the capital, Madison. Koshkonong, by Lake Koshkonong with a nucleus in Dane County but extending into Jefferson and Rock counties, founded in 1840, was perhaps, as Blegen claims, the most important of all the Wisconsin settlements. It was certainly the most prosperous.

Muskego, by Lake Muskego south of Milwaukee, founded in 1839, is likely the most noteworthy of the Norwegian pioneer settlements. The land selected was poor, similar to that of the ill-fated Beaver Creek colony in Illinois. But the settlers stayed, and the Muskego settlement was reinforced by continued immigration. It gained importance because so many newcomers stopped there on their way west. Its proximity to Milwaukee explains in part its significance; Milwaukee became a major gateway for immigrants to Wisconsin. The Muskego church, completed and dedicated in March 1845, is generally considered to be the first Norwegian Lutheran church in America. It is also noteworthy that the first Norwegian American newspaper, *Nordlyset*, made its appearance in Muskego in 1847. Muskego had a number of unusual leaders, which explains its central role in the Norwegian American community.

By the end of the 1840s, pioneer settlers migrated from Muskego and Koshkonong, and Norwegian land seekers began to settle in western Wisconsin. The coulee country along the Mississippi River, from Crawford County to Barron County, was in time an almost solid strip of Norwegian settlements. The well-known Coon Valley and Coon Prairie in Vernon County date from 1848. In the Trempealeau valley north of La Crosse, another Norwegian agricultural region came into being; La Crosse became a commercial and cultural center for the settlers. A large Norwegian settlement known as Indielandet began around 1850 in Portage and Waupaca counties in north-central Wisconsin. The pioneer settlers went first to the town of Scandinavia after a stop in Winnebago County. New and older settlements retained close relations, and a sense of Norwegian American commonality existed.

Canadian authorities competed for the newcomers, who were considered to be valuable settlers. An 1861 report by A. C. Buchanan, chief emigration agent at the port of Quebec, describes efforts "to secure the immigration of large numbers of Norwegians." Buchanan hoped that "a large number of these most industrious and valuable settlers," whose "fruits of industry is apparent wherever they locate themselves," would be brought over to Canada.

The Upper Midwest in general, but most obviously Wisconsin, had advantages in attracting Norwegian settlers; among these were the established Norwegian settlements in the state. Norwegian settlements were welcoming havens where newcomers could be made to feel at home. Even Quebec emigration agent Buchanan realized the allure of established settlements:

The Norwegian immigrants, as in previous years, have nearly all proceeded to the Western States. The large settlements of these people in Illinois and Wisconsin naturally tend to draw their countrymen around them: every vessel which arrives here has always a majority of her passengers who are coming out to join their friends, and who exercise an important influence upon the others. Those, just arrived in a strange country, and unacquainted with the language, naturally prefer to accompany their countrymen to encountering difficulties of which they have no proper knowledge, and which parties, from interested motives, are more inclined to exaggerate than otherwise.[17]

Official campaigns by Wisconsin and other states and propaganda by colonization agents, railroad and steamship companies, and other financial interests directed at the emigrants before their departure from the homeland and on their arrival in America were added inducements to locate in the Upper Midwest. An aggressive recruitment policy was conducted during the decades under consideration.

chapter 2

Timber and Emigrants

N orway is a coastal nation with a long seafaring tradition dating back to the age of the Vikings, when Norsemen explored Europe by its oceans and rivers for trade and conquest. Showing great seamanship, the Vikings ventured across the Atlantic in their versatile wooden longships. The Viking age represents an important facet of the medieval history of Scandinavia. It is viewed as a heroic age and a reminder to later generations of a longstanding maritime legacy.

This chapter considers the growth of the Norwegian merchant sailing fleet in the nineteenth century, an expansion that led historian Nils Vigeland to claim that the Norwegian sailing ships during that century conquered the seven oceans of the world. The trade in lumber and immigrants to Canada played a significant, even the primary, role in the escalating commercial operations, inaugurating and fostering the golden age of the Norwegian sailing fleet. Norway excelled in international maritime transport in a Scandinavian context as well. In 1879 Norway accounted for 5.6 percent of world tonnage, while the Swedish share was only 2.3 percent and Denmark held but 1.2 percent of the total.[1]

A VOYAGE TO QUEBEC

The sailing ship *Fædre Minde* left Christiania (Oslo) for Quebec City in Canada East on April 11, 1854, and anchored in Quebec harbor on June 2 after a strenuous voyage across the Atlantic lasting more than seven weeks. A man by the name of Ole Olson Østerud, one of a group of passengers from Hurdal, north of Oslo, wrote in detail to his brother in Norway from the Muskego settlement in Wisconsin on June 21, 1854.

Østerud was a mature man of thirty-four at the time of his emigration. A Lutheran pastor gave a farewell sermon as the emigrants boarded the ship. They sailed along the southern coast after departing from Oslo and then, Østerud relates, "northward toward Bergen, and on the fifteenth we saw the land of Norway the last time. The last we saw of Norway was high snow-capped mountains." Indeed, in the mid-nineteenth century, few immigrants would ever see Norway again. The final view would also be the final farewell to the homeland.

After passing the Shetland Islands, which sheltered the vessel from a storm, they entered the Atlantic Ocean in the morning of April 17. With favorable winds, they sailed about eleven miles in a watch, or a period of four hours. "On the first of May," Østerud tells his brother, "we had the most severe storm of the whole trip. It came from the northwest and later from the west, lasting until the fifth; then it was calm until evening, when a southwest wind arose, so that we made eleven miles in the watch." Østerud continues, recording that "We reached the Grand Bank of Newfoundland on the eighth of May, and there we fished on the eighth, ninth, and eleventh. We got seventy cod." The cod were ready to be caught. "It mattered not," Østerud writes, "whether one had bait, for few had bait on the hook. So the cod was really a fool."

In the morning of May 15, Captain A. Müller announced that he saw America, but dense fog hid the land and floating ice made it impossible to sail further until the twenty-fourth of May. The passengers saw land the morning of the twenty-seventh.

Three days later, about ten miles from the coast of Quebec, they saw land on both sides. "In the afternoon of June first," wrote Østerud, "we reached an island where a doctor lived." The island was Grosse Île, located in the St. Lawrence River some twenty-nine miles from Quebec City; it served as a quarantine station. All ships were required to stop at Grosse Île. The passengers were landed there, or a doctor would come on board and examine them. If there were no contagious diseases, the vessel might continue to Quebec harbor.

"There were," Østerud happily states, "no deaths on board *Fædre Minde*." The only illness was seasickness, but a child had been born. The vessel was allowed to land, and "at twelve o'clock on the third of June we stepped onto American soil for the first time." In reading the letter, one is struck by the passengers' dependence on nature and the elements.[2]

NORWAY AND EUROPE

Norway's remote geographic location at the northern periphery of the European continent might on one hand isolate the country from the great centers of culture and power in Europe, while its extended coastline on the other hand encouraged maritime connections west and south throughout its history. Before considering the growth and commerce of the Norwegian merchant sailing fleet, it is of basic import to shed light on Norway's early history and

Looking to Quebec from across the St. Lawrence River, this engraving from 1860 depicts a busy maritime scene. From the *Illustrated London News*, August 25, 1860. *Image courtesy of Bruce Weaver II*

the complex political events unfolding in the north at the beginning of the nineteenth century, during which Norway was reborn as a sovereign nation.

Unification has been a persistent theme in the history of the Nordic countries. The national decline in Norway that began in the late Middle Ages resulted in dynastic unions with Denmark and Sweden. Norway became the underdog in relationship to its two neighboring kingdoms. In 1380 Norway was drawn into a union with Denmark, which in 1397 expanded to include all three Nordic kingdoms in the so-called Kalmar Union, formed in that city at a meeting of the three Scandinavian national councils and greater nobles. For Norway the union was to last until 1814, and for Sweden until 1523.

Historical developments weakened Norway's position vis-à-vis Denmark. The Lutheran Reformation in 1536 strengthened royal power; Danish became the written language of Norway and deluged the spoken language for large sections of Norwegian society. That year the Danish king and Danish nobility decided to abolish the Norwegian council of the realm (*riksråd*). Norway, in the words of the charter of royal succession, was to become but a part of the realm of Denmark, situated under the Danish crown for time everlasting. Even though a complete integration into Denmark did not occur and a sense of Norwegian-ness persisted, Norway's instrument of national sovereignty was destroyed.

Agriculture was how most Norwegians made a living in the years 1500–1800. Even at the end of that period, at least 75 percent of the population received its main income from farming. There was a market on the continent for fish from the sea; the expanded fisheries and sales abroad made the Norwegian economy grow. In the 1500s the timber trade became important; like the fisheries, forestry was a Norwegian industry that could succeed only with demands from abroad.

The growth of Europe's population not only reduced the forested areas but simultaneously increased demand for wood products in the shipping and housing industries. The growing population around the North Sea turned to Norway, where the transport from its southern seaports was short and the supply extensive. Access to the forests was easiest along the coasts from the Oslofjord to Bergen; the large number of rivers and streams brought great advantage, for these could power the saws. Norway sold boards but also other timber products, such as beams. As the forests in the southern regions of western Norway were being depleted, the industry moved to Møre and Trøndelag. The resources along the coast of Agder and in eastern Norway were also exploited, and as a result tree felling moved inland. Most of Norway's growing fleet was occupied in carrying its exports, mainly fish and timber, to markets in western and southern Europe.

The first reliable census in 1801 sets the number of inhabitants at 880,000 at least. Norway's trade in lumber has a long history; prior to the Napoleonic Wars it was the country's most important export commodity. The shipping industry was to a high degree based on timber. Foreign and domestic developments in basic industries, mining and forestry, created resources that allowed for extensive import of grain and other provisions. Norway experienced a significant population growth that must be seen in connection with the increasing production and import of food items.

The collapse of the Danish-Norwegian union occurred, to quote historian Ståle Dyrvik, "because in the course of the 300 years after 1536, Norwegian society had grown large enough, rich enough and self-conscious enough to step into the ranks of independent states." There was in addition a governing elite, *embetsmenn*, to use the Norwegian term—lacking in 1536— that saw itself as Norwegian; these officials demanded a separate university and national bank and were supported by the lumber patricians in eastern Norway. A separate Norwegian awareness, to paraphrase Dyrvik, proved to be stronger than the close links with Denmark. The official class of *embetsmenn* was mainly instrumental in the establishment of a national Norwegian identity.

Denmark-Norway's involvement in the Napoleonic Wars created the events that led to the union's collapse. In August 1807, Great Britain, fearing that the Danish-Norwegian fleet would be taken over by Napoleon, sent a large combined land and sea force to Copenhagen. The town was besieged, and the fleet captured or destroyed. The Danish-Norwegian king readily allied the country with Napoleon, obligating Denmark-Norway to wage war along with France and Russia against Great Britain and its ally Sweden. The conflict with Great Britain hindered Norway's exports, restricted grain imports, and caused great difficulties for shipping. Food shortage and famine impacted much of eastern Norway in 1809. In 1810 the Swedish national assembly chose the French marshal, Jean-Baptiste Bernadotte, as crown prince, since King Carl XIII of Sweden had no heirs. Bernadotte became Crown Prince Carl Johan and played a decisive role in further developments. In November 1813, as commander of the Army of the North in the Battle of the Nations near Leipzig that had defeated Napoleon in October, Carl Johan decided to move his army north into Holstein. He drove back the Danish army and forced King Frederik VI of Denmark-Norway to sign the Treaty of Kiel on January 14, 1814. In the fourth paragraph of the treaty, Frederik, under the monarchical principle, ceded Norway to the king of Sweden.

Under the leadership of Danish crown prince Christian Frederik, who had been sent to Norway in 1813 as viceroy to frustrate the well-known Swedish plans to conquer the country, Norway rebelled against the Treaty of Kiel in defense of independence. The most decisive and cogent event was the Constitutional Convention at Eidsvoll. On April 10, 1814, 112 popularly elected representatives met in a national assembly there. On May 17 the assembly adopted a constitution based on popular sovereignty and the division of power, declared Norway's independence, and elected Christian Frederik king. The class of *embetsmenn* played a significant role at Eidsvoll; the governmental structure established by the constitution assured the official class a dominant position in both the executive and the legislative branches. This government by elite lasted more than fifty years. Norway was restored as an independent kingdom and had a constitution that, even though favoring the elite, gave political rights to, as historian Dyrvik writes, "an unusually wide spectrum of the people."

Norway had in an incredibly short time created national constitutional organs and moved from royal absolutism to liberal constitutional rule. Carl

Johan was, however, not ready to abandon the conditions of the Kiel Treaty. Already in April he appealed to his allies to enforce its terms and at the end of July sent Swedish troops into Norway. The war ended August 14 with the Moss Convention, where Carl Johan declared that he would accept the Eidsvoll constitution as a basis for negotiations. The Norwegian parliament established in the constitution, the Storting (Grand Assembly), convened in an extraordinary session on October 7. Christian Frederik abdicated, and the Storting revised the constitution to allow for a dynastic union with Sweden. On November 4 the elderly Carl XIII was elected to the Norwegian throne. Sweden and Norway had a common king and became the United Kingdoms. Norway preserved its domestic independence; in foreign policy Sweden was the dominant partner. It was precisely Norway's demand for a separate foreign consular service that led to the 1905 dissolution of the union. "The link to Sweden," as Dyrvik describes it, "was to last 90 years."[3]

A Maritime Tradition

In his work on "seamen's life in the era of sailing ships," maritime author Gøthe Gøthesen has the following summary: "Until 1850–60, the Norwegian sailing ship fleet by and large engaged in domestic trade. The west coast people sent their fish to the Baltic and Mediterranean and returned home with grain or salt. The vessels from southern and eastern Norway sailed with Norwegian and Swedish lumber to England, France, and Holland. On their voyage home they often sailed with ballast or from an English port with a cargo of coal."

The impressive growth in Norwegian shipping and economy during the years 1770 until 1807 was based on Norway's neutrality at a time when the rest of the world was drawn into destructive wars that upset all normal trading relationships. The good times ended when Denmark-Norway joined the conflict as an ally of Napoleon in 1807. In British ports alone, some three hundred Norwegian vessels were confiscated and a total crew of about three thousand men imprisoned. But in the long run, Britain could not do without lumber, and, in spite of war, Norwegian ships were given special passports or licenses to sail to England, beginning in July 1809 and lasting until 1813. During these years, the price of timber quintupled and brought about considerable commerce and the acquisition of new ships, but only in eastern Norway, since England had no use for the fish from western Norway.

In 1813 England enacted a nearly prohibitively high toll on the lumber trade; for Norway this toll destroyed the trade with that country. British colonies and, most significantly, Canada paid only one-tenth of the toll. Only in the 1840s was the toll reduced. Norwegian shipowners found profitable markets for Norwegian lumber by resuming the age-old trade with Holland and initiating trade with France. The latter especially compensated the port cities exporting lumber in South Norway for the loss of the English market.

The years after 1815 were nevertheless difficult for the Norwegian fleet; the depression following the war affected all industry. In addition, most countries adopted protectionism, similar to England's import toll on lumber. Norway, in order to export its main products—lumber, fish, and iron— advocated free trade; it became, as historian Vigeland maintains, "a virtue of necessity."[4]

The Norwegian fleet decreased in size from year to year until 1826; the timber trade from Swedish Baltic ports was thereafter open. Norwegian vessels soon captured this market and had a monopoly on it until the mid-1860s. Only then did the Swedes follow suit. Norwegian sailors were, according to Vigeland, leaders in the transport of timber, without doubt "The best in the world." He traces the growth of lumber transport "to all port cities in the world" as follows: "To begin with there was cargo only from Norwegian ports, later it was to sail with lumber from the port cities along the Baltic coast, Finnish ports, from the White Sea, and finally from Canada, Puget Sound and other places."

The fleet east of the municipality of Lindesnes on the southern tip of Norway transported timber. West of Lindesnes, fish was the basis for shipping. The cities of Stavanger and Bergen possessed a large fleet of smaller vessels that sailed to the Baltic with herring and returned home with cereals.

Bergen in addition had ships transporting fish to the Mediterranean, returning with cargoes of salt. In the mid-1850s, the Crimean War opened the
Black Sea for Norwegian sailing ships with new and expanding transport
of cargo. The Norwegian merchant fleet enjoyed unbroken growth from
1826 until 1879; it in fact quintupled in tonnage. New ships were built or
purchased; these were both better constructed and larger than those of the
old fleet. Norwegian shipping firms took advantage of all possibilities and
expanded the fleet's field of action from year to year.[5]

A Change in Destination

The Norwegian sailing fleet owed its initial expansion to the trade in lumber
and emigrants with Canada beginning in 1850. "The great dividing line in
the history of our merchant fleet is in reality 1850. Then our golden age
begins," historian Jacob S. Worm-Müller maintains. The victory for free
trade in Great Britain with the repeal of the Navigation Acts may be seen as
the foremost factor in liberating world trade; it began an economic revolution that had far-reaching consequences for commercial activity worldwide.

The British Navigation Acts were a series of laws that formed the basis
for overseas trade for nearly two hundred years; the laws under the economic
theory of mercantilism restricted the use of foreign shipping for trade
between Britain and its colonies. The timber trade from Canada to Great
Britain was an important economic factor on both sides of the Atlantic.
Historian Robert Bothwell writes, "Timber flowed to Great Britain, and
timber ships sailed back crammed with immigrants—slowly at first, but in
huge numbers after the middle of the 1820s." Norwegian sailing ships were
free to engage in this lucrative trade beginning in 1850.[6]

Repeal of the Navigation Acts became effective January 1, 1850, but already
the previous year the Norwegian ship *Flora* from Tønsberg was reported to
be on its way from Quebec to London with timber, deals, and staves, having
been chartered in New York in September. Norwegian shipowners responded
quickly to the new opportunities. "The voyage of *Flora*," historian Helge
Nordvik points out, "heralded a new epoch in Norwegian shipping; the

beginning of large-scale transatlantic trade and shipping between third countries." The Norwegian fleet achieved a leading position among the world's shipping nations.

The sustained flow of Norwegian immigrants during the ensuing decades, with Quebec the main port of entry, laid the foundation for strong Norwegian participation in the Canadian wood trade. Linking the emigrant and timber trades enabled Norwegian vessels to capture an ever-larger market share of the trade centered on the ports of the St. Lawrence. As early as 1850, George Pemberton, acting Swedish-Norwegian consul in Quebec, reported that "the number of vessels from Norway considerably exceeds that from any other foreign country." Norwegian ships continued to constitute the largest number of non-British foreign vessels arriving at the port of Quebec; in 1872, they totaled 15.6 percent. The vast majority sailed to Canada in ballast to return to Great Britain with timber. In 1850 only two of the twelve sailing vessels landing in the port of Quebec from Norway carried emigrants.

The emigration agent in Quebec City, A. C. Buchanan, in his 1850 report noted that the first parties of Norwegians to ever arrive at the port had made the voyage on the ship *Lyna* and the bark *Benedicte*, both departing from Drammen in June and arriving at their destination in late summer.

There was some public confusion about the benefits of landing in Quebec. In its issue for June 8, 1850, *Drammens Adresse*, in reporting the departure of *Lyna*, criticizes its rival *Drammens Tidende* for claiming that "this landing place must be less convenient for the passengers destined for the Norwegian colonies in the interior." *Drammens Adresse*'s response included the following: "If *Drammens Tidende* had investigated the case (which should have been its simple duty) before it dared to insult the shipowners of *Lyna*, it would have found out that they had the word of an agent in Quebec, that passengers could travel daily with steamship to Buffalo. The traveling time is only 2½ to 3 days while the traveling time from New York to Buffalo is 5 to 6 days."

Drammens Adresse correctly predicted that "In the future, it will probably happen that the emigrant ships will set their course toward Quebec rather than to New York." All passengers on both vessels proceeded directly to

Chicago by steamer to Lewiston on the lower Niagara River and then by train to Buffalo and from there to Chicago. They numbered 224 and were according to the report chiefly farmers headed for Norwegian settlements in Wisconsin. These emigrants spearheaded a rapidly increasing flow of Norwegians looking for a new life on the other side of the Atlantic. Buchanan also stated that one-half of the emigrant head tax was refunded under the provisions of a recently enacted law allowing such refunds to emigrants who certified their intention to continue directly to the United States.

In his study of the Norwegian immigration to North America, historian Lars Erik Larson points to three key factors that explain the abrupt shift of the Norwegian emigrant stream from New York to Quebec. The first one discouraged emigrants from landing in New York. The United States and the state of New York enacted laws in the 1840s that substantially increased fares. The laws passed by Congress in the late 1840s imposed costly and strict requirements, according to Larson, "for passenger space, food and water, cooking and toilet facilities, and ventilation and sanitation on all passenger vessels arriving in the United States." New York State in 1847 approved a law for a capitation tax of one dollar per emigrant, raised in following years, and a bonding requirement of three hundred dollars per emigrant, assessed to the vessel owner. "The purpose of the bonding requirement," Larson states, "was to encourage ship owners and masters to transport only healthy and vigorous passengers and to care for them during the voyage, and to pay for the expense of caring for sick and indigent passengers."

The fares to Quebec on ships going to Canada from Norway for cargoes of timber were much lower than for emigrants traveling to New York. The Canada trade provided cargo in both directions, though the vast majority of vessels, as stated above, sailed in ballast to engage in the transportation of timber.

The second factor was the distance from Quebec to Norwegian settlements in the Upper Midwest, where the majority of immigrants were headed, which was, as *Drammens Adresse* reminded its readers, shorter and cheaper than from New York. The network of steamer and rail routes which by 1850

carried the emigrants westward constituted a third factor; this route will be
more fully explored in chapter four. A triangular trade between Norway,
Canada, and Great Britain was in place for Norwegian emigrants beginning
in the 1850s; it made available passenger space and low fares.

Norway became the most important foreign shipping nation in the
Canadian timber trade. "There was a reddening of Norwegian flags in most
of the ports in the St. Lawrence River that exported timber," A. N. Kiær,
director of the Norwegian Central Bureau of Statistics, stated. Vessels sailing in ballast, which might include iron wares from Sweden or Norway, and
seeking cargoes of timber, might land in Quebec City; timber of all kinds
arrived there to be transported to the British Isles. Quebec City remained the
main port of entry for Norwegian immigrants, although some also landed
in Montreal. Sailing ships docked in great numbers at the many smaller
seaports in the St. Lawrence waterway to load timber, and some of these
vessels had passengers. Only a few Norwegian immigrants, however, landed
at such port cities as St. John in New Brunswick, Halifax in Nova Scotia,
and Gaspé in Gaspésie. Detailed information in regard to these seaports
is missing.[7]

THE EMIGRATION

Norwegian official statistics chronicle the spread of emigration in the homeland and the destinations overseas. Norwegian immigrants to America before
1850, as recounted in chapter one, may be viewed as the forerunners of the
mass overseas movement of people in the second half of the nineteenth
century. The dramatic crossing of the sloop *Restauration* in 1825 launched the
transport of Norwegian emigrants by sailing ships from ports in Norway.
Heavy passenger traffic to North America on Norwegian sailing ships would
last into the mid-1870s. Annual emigration began only in 1836, however, even
though individuals had crossed the Atlantic in the interim. Starting the
following year, 1837, there was an increasing volume. The great number of
emigrants from 1836 to 1850, as Theodore Blegen notes, followed routes that
brought them to New York, Boston, or other American ports either by

direct passage on a Norwegian vessel or by way of Hamburg, Le Havre, or Liverpool.

Official Norwegian statistics have a total of 18,200 immigrants in the period 1836 to 1850; 95 percent left in the years 1840 to 1850, rising from 300 in 1840 to 3,700 in 1850. The highest point was in 1849, when 4,000 Norwegians emigrated. These numbers deviate somewhat from American statistics on arrivals. According to Director Kiær, about 12,200 of the 18,200 Norwegian immigrants went directly from Norway to America on a Norwegian sailing vessel; of these about 11,960 landed at U.S. ports and, as suggested earlier, 240 at Quebec. About 6,000 went via the more important European emigration ports outside Norway.[8]

The rise of the St. Lawrence route beginning in 1850 meant that New York would to a large extent lose its standing as the main port of entry for Norwegian immigrants to North America for more than twenty years. The shift in destination came about during the years 1851 and 1852, when 7,500 immigrants went directly from Norway to Quebec. The two years represent a transitional period in which the direct shipping from Norway, as Blegen points out, "reduces emigration by way of other European countries and Quebec receives a larger proportion of the total Norwegian emigration than New York and other American ports." During these two years, in comparison, 4,550 emigrants crossed from Norway to New York and Boston and 660 left from a different European port, mainly Liverpool, the top choice of those who traveled indirectly in the 1850s. Some emigrants also went by way of Le Havre, Hamburg, or other ports to New York. From then on the balance shifted completely.

In the course of the years 1854 to 1865, as many as 44,100 Norwegian emigrants landed in Quebec; only 520 arrived in New York directly from Norway, and 2,280 traveled the indirect route via a European port city. During these years, then, 94 percent of all Norwegian immigrants to North America entered through the port of Quebec—a significant number of people in this first great wave in the overseas exodus. Indicative of the substantial numbers of Norwegians who were arriving is the appointment of Norwegian-born

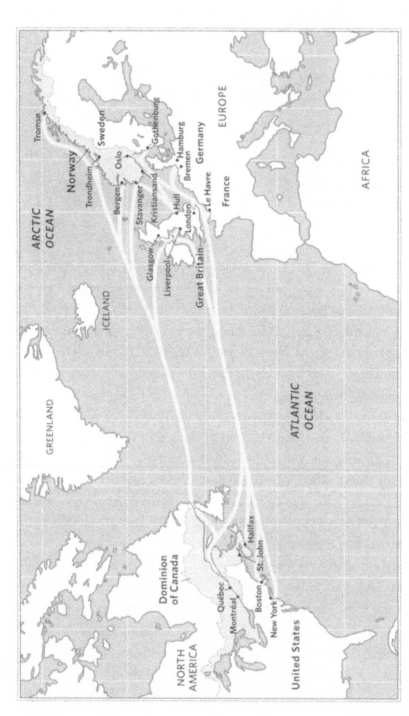

Across the Deep Sea. *Drawn by Matt Kania*

A. Jorgensen as interpreter for the Canadian immigration office. In 1865 Jorgensen published a most informative circular titled "Emigration from Europe during the Present Century: Its Causes and Effects." Most of it was translated from Norwegian official reports, and it deals with the Norwegian and the European movement overseas in general. Jorgensen became active in agitating for Norwegian settlements in Canada. He notes that, by 1865, 48,060 Norwegians had arrived in Canada. The earlier cited figures are based on official Norwegian statistics; the figures in the Swedish-Norwegian consular reports, consulted by Helge Nordvik and Lars Erik Larson in their studies, differ slightly from Norwegian statistics, with somewhat lower numbers. Both sources show a drop in arrivals during the American Civil War. The consular figures show a decline from 8,406 in 1861 to 4,949 the following year, and to only 987 in 1863.

The 1866 figures give evidence of the beginning of the post–Civil War mass migration—1866 to 1874—with 13,006 Norwegian emigrants still landing in Quebec, but it declined thereafter. The year 1874 saw the final arrival of emigrants on Norwegian sailing vessels directly from Norway, a total of only 506 people. The number of Norwegians who arrived in the port of Quebec directly from Norway from 1850 to 1874 amounted to 114,852. These figures cover only those who arrived on sailing ships directly from Norway. Steamship arrivals are not included. This total equals about 68 percent of all Scandinavians who landed in Quebec in the same period. Norway's total overseas migration in the same time span was 178,907; in these years, then, for about 64 percent of all Norwegian overseas emigrants Quebec was the port of entry.

New York was gradually reclaiming its place as the main destination for Norwegian emigrants to North America and received nearly all of those not landing in Quebec. The United Kingdoms' consular reports from Quebec and New York for 1872 registered 4,940 Norwegian arrivals in Quebec and 6,451 in New York; the following year the respective figures were 3,079 and 6,066. After the Norwegian emigrant trade to Quebec came to an end in 1874, sailing ships crossed in ballast to Canada and transported lumber back across the Atlantic. In fact, in the years that followed, Norwegian sailing ships continued to increase their dominance in the timber trade to British North America, alongside the well-established Baltic trade. An era in Norwegian passenger traffic had ended, however. Steamships thereafter ruled supreme in overseas passenger traffic. In 1875 no Norwegian emigrant crossed over to America on a sailing ship; all emigrants from then on found berth on a transatlantic passenger steamer. And some Norwegian emigrants still continued to land in Quebec, rather than in New York, on British liners from Liverpool.[9]

The Regional Impulse and Information

Causes of immigration are regularly sought in a broad analysis of differing and shifting social and economic circumstances. In considering macro causalities and the statistical dimensions of the migration, one must, however, not disregard the human factor and the many individual motives and circumstances that influenced people to seek their fortunes outside the homeland. The resolve to emigrate was for the individual a matter of personal choice. One person might be the decisive voice for an entire family or other affiliated groups. Regardless, individuals responded with forethought to the forces and circumstances that encouraged emigration.

Statistical sources give a macro view of the overseas exodus. In order to capture the full drama of the emigration, it is necessary to consider individual emigrant experiences. As described in *The Promise of America*, "In a survey of the emigration the human factor may easily disappear in numbers, tables, and graphs; statistics only indicate the dimensions of the movement. It is therefore important to bear firmly in mind that the resolve to emigrate represented for the individual a personal decision."

During what may be described as the founding phase, from 1825 to 1865, 77,873 Norwegians crossed the Atlantic to make a home for themselves in America. To these figures may be added the 115,497 Norwegians who left during the first wave of mass migration, 1866–74. In these nearly fifty years, then, official Norwegian statistics registered 191,370 overseas departures; about 92 percent left between 1851 and 1874.[10]

Norway's Administrative Districts. *Drawn by Matt Kania*

Norwegians were pulled into the Atlantic economy and its patterns of trade and migration, as evidenced by the much-celebrated crossing of the Sloopers in 1825. They all hailed from the present *fylke* (province) of Rogaland on the southwestern coast of Norway, mainly from the community of Tysvær and a few from the city of Stavanger. As noted earlier, they sought religious freedom in the new land, but like later emigrants they also held out hope for economic advancement. Norwegian emigrants are in general seen as economic migrants. They were not refugees or escapees from famine, but in the main emigrated for the purpose of seeking better employment and an improved financial position. In addition to the financial prospects, there was also the greater freedom and social equality of the new land. There is no doubt that, at the moment the decision to emigrate was made, the hope for a better future for oneself and one's children was of utmost importance. America was the land of promise and opportunity, a powerful image throughout the era of emigration.

After the beginning of annual emigration in 1836, the urge to go to America spread like a dangerous disease—indeed, an "America fever"—from the southwestern coastal region, where it had begun, to coastal districts farther north and to the valleys of the interior. The communities in Ryfylke, a landscape on the Boknafjord in the inner part of Rogaland *fylke*, had many emigrants already from 1836. Between 1856 and 1865, the first decade when statistics on emigration intensity exist, 3,112 emigrants left Rogaland, for an annual average of 6.6 per one thousand inhabitants. The impulse to leave moved on to Hordaland *fylke* and the strikingly beautiful scenery around the Hardangerfjord and on to Voss. The emigration affected the different districts unevenly.

The timing of information about and knowledge of the opportunities offered—and drawbacks encountered—across the sea might explain the uneven spread of the immigration. While emigration from Voss flourished, the exodus from Hardanger stalled after discouraging information was transmitted. As early as 1836, emigrants from Ullensvang in Hardanger emigrated; in 1839 a group of twenty-two left Ulvik in Hardanger, arriving in Chicago on August 25 after a long and difficult journey. They suffered much hardship, and many in the group got sick and died. The men found employment, as historian George Flom reported, "some on the [Illinois and Michigan] canal, some on a schooner on the river, others in forestry around Chicago." Three of the emigrants, Brynjulf Lekve and the brothers Anders and Johan Vik, gave an account of their adversity and tribulations, advising people against coming to America. Their warning was printed in *Bergens Statstidende* on June 11, 1841. No emigrants from Hardanger protested the negative information. Flom maintains that this report was the reason why emigration from Hardanger discontinued until 1846 and why so few later emigrants from Hardanger settled in Chicago.

One should of course not assume that negative information from emigrated neighbors and kin gives a complete explanation of developments in Hardanger, though these details cannot be overlooked. One must also consider local factors, such as the total migration from the district, in order to understand the lacuna in the overseas movement. Another consideration is the increasing agitation against emigration by Norwegian officials from the end of the 1830s. The published report sent back to Norway by the three emigrants from Hardanger became part of the anti-emigration campaign. The authorities viewed with great concern the expansion of the overseas movement and in their propaganda against it made use of letters and other writings from dissatisfied emigrants in America.

The idea to seek a better future in America might have been planted by an individual, an innovator, based on news from America. The innovators in general belonged to the Norwegian farming class. The most important information about America was transmitted in letters from established earlier emigrants, and as seen above had a negative as well as a positive impact on the overseas exodus. These so-called "America letters," with their personal observations from people who had the confidence of the home community, played an important part in the entire emigrant movement. The arrival of an immigrant letter became an important event in the community. The letters were copied and recopied and circulated widely among neighbors and sent among parishes. In total, the letters created a positive picture of America, and some became an indictment of Norwegian class prejudices and the specific social and economic conditions at the root of the decision to emigrate. But they also provided matter-of-fact information about prospects and warned against coming to America when circumstances were less than promising. The letters made potential emigrants sensitive to the shifting economic conditions and events in America. These details might in part explain the annual fluctuations in the number of people emigrating. The rate of emigration was greatly influenced by economic conditions—good and bad times—both in Norway and in America. The depression in America that began in 1837 was reported in correspondence from disillusioned Norwegian settlers to those still in Norway; the consequence was a decline in the number of immigrants. The American Civil War, as noted, and the war with Dakota Indians in Minnesota in regions settled by Norwegians were clear factors in reducing the stream of immigrants in the 1860s.

The letters by Gjert G. Hovland, cited earlier, were copied by the hundreds and created great interest in the 1830s and 1840s and later as well. On July 9, 1842, Hovland wrote, "Hardly a day passes without my reflecting on how richly God blesses this country every year; and then my heart is moved to pity when my thoughts go back to Norway and I recall the poor people in cities and in the country who had to beg for the bare necessities of life with tears in their eyes. How happy the poor and the landless would consider themselves if they were here, especially those who are honest in purpose and cheerful."

Most letters were, of course, written by less-well-known men and women. They streamed back to Norway and had great effect on the genesis of emigration from individual parishes. Knowledge of America frequently became the final incentive to leave. Successful Norwegian Americans who visited the homeland were by their mere presence evidence of the opportunities that existed overseas. On their way back to America, they might serve as guides for groups of emigrants. The America guides, or "America books," as they were dubbed, represented another major source of information. They provided more complete and systematic details than did letters. They were eagerly read by people who intended to emigrate. The account by A. Jorgensen falls

Conditions were crowded on the small farms in the Norwegian fjord and mountain districts. These tradition-bound farming communities were not able to increase production to keep pace with the rapid growth in population, and pursuing a better life in America became the solution for many. *Norsk folkemuseum, Oslo, Norway*

into this category, but there were earlier guides like Ole Rynning's *Sandfærdig beretning om Amerika til oplysning og nytte for bonde og menigmand* (True Account of America for the Enlightenment and Benefit of the Peasant and the Common), published in Norway in 1838, and *Veiviser for norske emigranter til De forenede nordamerikanske stater og Texas* (Pathfinder for Norwegian Emigrants to the United States and Texas), published by Johan R. Reiersen in 1844, following a visit to America to study conditions there as the representative of some people who wanted to emigrate.

WEST NORWAY NORTHWARD

The district of Voss in Hordaland *fylke* had an early start and experienced major emigration, becoming the most distinct emigration district within that province. Among the first to emigrate from Voss was Nils Knutson Røthe, his wife Torbjørg, and their three children; they left in 1836 and got passage from Gothenburg on a ship carrying a cargo of iron for America. They settled in frontier Chicago. They were later joined by a steady stream of emigrants from Voss. By 1845 the Chicago newspaper the *Daily Democrat* could report that "the Norwegians are crowding to this city by hundreds." It was a rural to urban migration, not rural to rural, which was the most common settlement pattern. The immigrants found gainful employment in Chicago. Many Norwegians got work on the Illinois and Michigan Canal, which opened in 1848. The early Norwegian colony owed much to the canal, the construction of which, with its accompanying possibility of employment, attracted many nationalities to the city.

In 1848 the Vossings in Chicago organized the Vossing Correspondence Society (*Det vossiske korrespondance Selskab*) to give "systematic enlightenment to the Norwegian people concerning the status of their emigrated compatriots and to refute false assertions regarding America and the Norwegian immigrants." The society was founded in response to the negative report given by the Swedish-Norwegian consul general Adam Løvenskjold in New York to the Norwegian government after his visit to Norwegian settlements in the Midwest in the summer of 1847. His report was published in Bergen in 1848 and reprinted in several newspapers. Unlike the situation for the Hardanger emigrants in Chicago, the action taken by the Vossings appears to have saved the day. Several hundred people from Voss crossed the Atlantic in 1850. A second factor worked to the same end. The year before, in 1849, three successful pioneer emigrants, then residing in Chicago, had visited Voss to speed up emigration; among these was Ivar Larson Bøe, who as a civic leader and prosperous businessman in Chicago became Iver Lawson. In 1856 Chicago Vossings organized the Vossing Emigration Society (*Det vossiske Emigrationsselskab*), the object of which was "to collect funds through free subscription to be used simply and only to help needy and deserving families to America." The correspondence society merged with the new organization. In the years 1856 and 1857, nearly three hundred people emigrated from Voss. Both societies illustrate actions taken by emigrated compatriots in promoting movement from their home communities in Norway. Outside Chicago, Vossings settled widely in rural Norwegian settlements.[11]

Between 1856 and 1865, present-day Sogn og Fjordane *fylke* in western Norway, in Norwegian known as Vestlandet, lost a larger proportion of its population than any other Norwegian province, 6,430 in all; 96 percent of the total were from Sogn in the south, mainly from the central and inner communities on the Sognefjord, which had an exceptionally high rate of emigration. In 1856 Sogn had a population of 38,203; 61 percent resided in the central and inner part of the district. Between 1856 and 1865 the annual average number of emigrants equaled 17.2 per one thousand of the median population. From 1865 to 1895 another 14,500 left for America from Sogn, but this indicated a lower rate of emigration. For the entire *fylke* the rate fell to 10.4 per one thousand population between 1866 and 1875. The parish of Vik was greatly affected by the overseas exodus, and the movement struck early. In 1839 Per Ivarson Undi, a farmer from Vik, left as the first emigrant from the *fylke* with his wife, Anna, and two children.

The emigration from the district of Sogn is closely related to the earlier one from its neighbor to the south and demonstrates how the "America fever" spread northward along the coast, in this case through family connections. Per Undi's wife, Anna Skjervheim, was from the community of Myrkdalen in Voss; two of her brothers had emigrated from there in 1837. Peder Skjervheim encouraged Per Undi to join him in America, as Undi and his family did in 1839. That same year a large number of people emigrated from Voss.

As historian Rasmus Sunde observes, Undi "led the way, not only across the ocean but also into what was then the distant West." Letters from Wiota, Wisconsin, from Undi and his brother, who emigrated in 1841, strongly urged relatives and neighbors to join them in America. Undi was well situated in Vik and prospered in the New World. He wrote to the home community regarding the wisdom of moving overseas: "As you are in such doubts and wish to hear the full truth from Per Undi and his wife whether they ever regretted leaving—well, here both of them stand and declare that they thank the good Lord who gave them the desire and courage to leave their farm and seek their fortune in America where they have found life more comfortable than in Norway." Thereafter, people from Vik and other parts of Sogn left for America. In 1843 30 people emigrated from Vik, in 1844, 103, and in 1845, 111. They were the vanguard of the large exodus beginning in the following decade. *Christiania-Posten* reported in 1854 that there were hardly any families in inner Sogn that did not have several members who had emigrated to America. During these same years, 223 people emigrated from other districts in Sogn.[12]

The emigration from the two northern districts of Sogn og Fjordane *fylke*, Sunnfjord and Nordfjord, was never large. During the years 1856–65, when Sogn lost 17.2 per thousand of its median population annually through emigration, the two northern districts had scattered cases. Only 226 left the two northern districts, while, as indicated above, 6,430 emigrated from Sogn in the same decade. Not until 1866 did Sunnfjord get involved in the overseas movement, with the exception of the community of Jølster in Sunnfjord, from which groups left in 1864. The herring fishery in the coastal regions prospered during the 1850s and 1860s, attracting fishermen from all over Norway as well as giving the local population an income. It also provided resources to emigrate or move to other parts of Norway. Bergen became the main destination for those who left Sunnfjord. Internal migration, in this case established connections to an urban center, made overseas migration less likely.

In general, districts that had new industry and livelihoods or whose residents had possibilities for income in other regions within Norway had a relatively small overseas emigration. Historian Ingrid Semmingsen points to the historic fact that, while some communities sent their entire population surplus to America, others experienced an equal division between overseas emigration and internal migration. Present-day Møre og Romsdal had a relatively late beginning, and in the decade 1866 to 1875 had the lowest rate of emigration of all provinces—1.9 emigrants per thousand of its median population. The flourishing coastal cities and the prosperous fisheries created a shortage of labor, and as a result wages rose, attracting workers from the inland districts of Norway and the mountain communities in the Gudbrandsdalen valley.

TRØNDELAG AND NORTH NORWAY

Emigration from the provinces of Nord-Trøndelag and Sør-Trøndelag began later than in the southern regions of Norway, in spite of the 1837 emigration of Hans Barlien and Ole Rynning from Nord-Trøndelag; Rynning, author of the influential guidebook *True Account of America*, left from Snåsa, and Barlien, who emigrated at the advanced age of sixty-five, from Overhalla in Namdalen. In letters back home, Barlien praised America, contrasting the superior conditions there to those he disliked in the homeland. In an 1839 letter he concluded, "Tell all who would like to know that I am as contented as any human being can be, and anyone who wants to come over will with little effort become just as happy."

According to official statistics, 150 people emigrated from Nord-Trøndelag between 1846 and 1855, in the following ten years 1,885 left, and from 1866 to 1875 those departing numbered 6,097, equal to an annual rate of 7.4 per thousand of the median population. Historian Jostein Molde points to flaws in the official numbers before the emigration records started in 1867. The number of emigrants from Sør-Trøndelag, again from official statistics, amounted to only 90 between 1846 and 1855, increasing to 279 in 1856–65, and to 6,037 in the ten years thereafter, for an annual rate per thousand of 5.3. Some 1,300 people left from the city of Trondheim between 1846 and 1875.

By 1855 all of Norway's nineteen provinces (Troms became the twentieth province in 1866), with the exception of Nordland, participated in the exodus, albeit with great variations. In the next decade, every Norwegian administrative unit engaged in the overseas movement. Nordland *fylke* was a receiving region within Norway, with migration from the south; most of those who moved sought land, but an added draw was the north's profitable cod fishery, "an America for many," as Semmingsen claims. During the five years 1846–50, as an example, of the 1,117 people who left Sogn, 840 emigrated to America, 220 moved to Nordland, and 57 relocated to Møre og Romsdal. Between 1820 and 1865, 250 people from Voss moved to Nordland or Troms. People from regions with restricted agricultural land generally migrated to northern Norway or to the herring and cod fisheries in western Norway. Then America fever took hold, and overseas migration replaced this internal movement.

The history of the Bardu and Målselv valleys in Troms *fylke* is an especially illustrative example of internal migration. The movement north to the two large valleys began in the late 1700s from northern Østerdalen and Gudbrandsdalen and then spread to the province of Nord-Trøndelag, which was a resting place on the way north for the migrants. The Norwegian census records 58 people in the Bardu valley in 1801, ten families residing on as many farmsteads. By 1845 Bardu's population had increased to 536. Thereafter, the influx from southern Norway declined because "migrants increasingly preferred the fertile, uncultivated prairies of the American Midwest over Norway's bleak northern lands." The America fever raged not only in the districts that had sent their surplus population north but in Bardu itself, which experienced a large overseas exodus. The first Bardudøls left as early as 1852; in the course of the next three years, forty more people went to America. The migration overseas continued with strength in the following decades.

The early Bardu emigrants had taken a coastal steamship and found berths on a sailing ship from a port city farther south, generally from Bergen; beginning in 1857, emigrant ships departed also from Trondheim. One must assume that there were Bardudøls as well among the 589 emigrants—a strikingly large number—from Troms who in 1864 crossed the Atlantic from the city of Tromsø to Quebec on two large sailing ships that had traveled north from Bergen.

According to the newspaper *Tromsø Stiftstidende*, among the emigrants there were many religious dissenters, dissatisfied with the ecclesiastical situation in Norway. A number of religious movements were especially visible in the fast-growing town of Tromsø. Two in particular played a role in the emigration to North America. Læstadianism was a widespread Lutheran religious lay movement in the northern regions of Finland, Sweden, and Norway. It was founded by Lars Levi Læstadius (1800–1861), a pastor in the Swedish Lutheran state church, after a personal conversion in 1844; he thereafter started a conservative Lutheran revival movement in north Sweden. The Læstadian faith was brought to Norway at the end of the 1840s, spread by Finnish- and Sami-speaking preachers. The movement gained many converts in the Sami and Kven populations; from the 1860s it increasingly became a Finnish movement. Kvens identify a population group that migrated from northern Finland to northern Norway in the 1800s.

Historian Hans Eirik Aarek, an authority on the history of Quakers in Norway, has studied the little-known small group of Norwegian Friends in northern Norway, mainly in Målselv and Tromsø. Between 1853 and 1896, there were eight visits to the region by foreign Quaker missionaries and their Norwegian companions. Asbjørn Kloster, the champion of teetotalism and head of a private Quaker school in Stavanger, was among the visitors to the north in 1855. Their work bore fruit as membership requests began to arrive in Stavanger. The Troms Friends never became members of the Society of Friends in Norway. They were too far from Stavanger, and their close relationship to the Free Apostolic Church was considered an impediment as well. The church represented the strong lay movement and religious awaking of the 1850s referred to as "Lammers' revival," from the Lutheran pastor Gustav Adolph Lammers (1802–78), who on July 2, 1856, left his pastorate in Skien and the Norwegian Lutheran state church; he founded a free apostolic congregation in that city. The Free Apostolic Church, however, dates from September 9, 1856, when the first congregation was founded in Tromsø a few days before that of the Skien congregation; a third was founded the same year in Balsfjord, and a few other congregations were organized in the vicinity during the next years. Lammers referred to the congregations in Tromsø and Balsfjord as impulses for his own lay activity, and the following year, 1857, he visited Tromsø. Several members of the Free Apostolic Church later became Quakers.

There were fifteen adult Quakers in Tromsø in 1860, in addition to children, and twelve in Målselv. Further, a number of people had contact with
the Quakers without being converted. Quaker converts were also found
on Kvaløy Island and at Lerstrand, some fourteen miles from Tromsø, and
at the town of Vardø in eastern Finnmark *fylke*. But emigration to America
caught on quickly. Between 1861 and 1863, most found voyage on sailing
ships to Quebec and Gaspé. Religious conditions and greater opportunity
were incitements to emigration. A letter dated March 1863 from the Quaker
Society in Stavanger to the Meeting for Suffering of Friends in Norway
that convened in London relates that only three Friends remained in Tromsø,
almost all were gone from Lerstrand, while in Målselv "a meeting continues
to be kept up by six or seven persons."

The few families leaving the Lofoten islands in Nordland *fylke* and Tromsø
and surrounding districts in Troms *fylke* in 1861, like the earlier Bardu emigrants, took a steamer south to Trondheim or Bergen and continued overseas
from there on a sailing vessel. The desire to leave increased substantially in
following years, leading *Tromsø Statstidende* to report on December 23, 1863,
that many people in Tromsø and nearby parishes were preparing to emigrate. Ingrid Semmingsen cites this passage from the newspaper: "Last year
and the year before there were to be sure few individuals among the city's
craftsmen and labor force who were totally untouched by America's attractions, and from the countryside emigrated not only newcomers from southern Norway but also native northerners, yes even some Sami fishermen made
their way to Wisconsin and Minnesota."

Troms *fylke* lost 1,418 citizens to emigration during the decade 1866 to
1875, for an annual emigration rate of 2.9 per thousand inhabitants. Nordland *fylke* had an identical rate in the same period based on a total departure
of 2,807 emigrants. The northernmost *fylke*, Finnmark, had, considering the
size of its population, a considerable overseas exodus. During the same years
2,142 people left, equal to an annual rate of emigration per thousand of 9.6;
about 730 had emigrated before 1866. Alta became a center of the movement
mainly due to a steady reduction in the operation of the copper works at

Kåfjord. A few workers left early, in 1862 and 1863, for the copper mines in Michigan, and as many as eighty people, adults and children, left in 1866. Finnmark's administrative center of Vadsø, on the Varanger Peninsula, became a major emigration area; as many as 673 left the town during the five years 1871–75, causing a population decline.

Many of the emigrants from Alta and from Finnmark in general were Kvens and converts to Læstadianism. Even though they did not leave the Norwegian Lutheran state church, as the Quakers and members of the Free Apostolic Church did, they met much opposition from the established church and faced a strict Norwegianization process both in school and church. The threat Norwegian authorities felt from Russia and Finland made them look upon differences between religious and ethnic groups with suspicion; in the case of Læstadianism, ethnic and religious differences joined forces. Michigan became the most common destination for the emigrants from Finnmark.

As historian Einar Niemi has shown, agents recruited Norwegians for the Michigan copper mines. Christian Taftezon is a remarkably early example. Before emigrating some time before 1864, he was well known in Finnmark, having served as sheriff in Vadsø. Taftezon made contact with the local management of the Quincy Mining Company in Upper Michigan and the Mining Emigrant Aid Association and helped develop the idea of contracting mining labor in Europe. The Læstadian revival movement preserved the language of the Finnish immigrants to Norway, the Kvens, and when they emigrated to America they took their form of Christianity with them in the Finnish language. The migratory tradition they created gained ground, and well into the twentieth century the mines in Upper Michigan were a major destination for Arctic Finns from northern Norway.[13]

EAST NORWAY

As noted in chapter one, the impulse to go to America reached East Norway, Østlandet, in 1837. Emigration had its point of origin in western Norway, in Rogaland *fylke* and Hordaland *fylke*, but the eastern districts nevertheless made the largest contribution to the movement as early as the 1840s.

The eastern provinces of Buskerud and Telemark were smitten by America fever. The communities in Hallingdal in Buskerud *fylke* were greatly affected; Hallings were encouraged to emigrate, as it was said, by Ole Rynning's America guide and a letter from an earlier emigrant. Up to 1875, more than 20,000 people moved overseas from Buskerud; in the ten years between 1866 and 1875, when 9,968 emigrated, it equaled an annual emigration of 9.9 per thousand of the median population. The brothers Ole and Ansten Nattestad, from Numedal in Buskerud *fylke*, as noted in chapter one, left for America in 1837 with a large group of emigrants, fifty-nine in all, mainly from Tinn in Telemark *fylke* and a few from Numedal. This, the so-called Rue party, was the first group migration from eastern Norway. Gjert Hovland's letters were well known in Tinn; the communities in Upper Telemark had close connections to western Norway. By 1875 some 21,630 Telemarkings had moved overseas; in the years 1866 through 1875, the 8,567 who departed equaled an annual emigration per thousand of 10.3. Telemark had one of the highest emigrations in terms of numbers and rates of any district in Norway. Amateur historian Hjalmar Rued Holand claimed that "Tinn in Upper Telemark has sent out more immigrants to America than any other community in Norway with the possible exception of Luster in Sogn."

  The desire to begin a new life in America spread to Oppland *fylke*, adjoining Hallingdal, which became another major region of emigration. The district of Land in the southern part of the province had considerable emigration in the 1840s. Lars Røste, the pioneer emigrant from the district who in 1839 had joined the Nattestad brothers, is credited with bringing the America fever to Land. He founded a colony of Landings in Wisconsin west of the Norwegian settlement at Jefferson Prairie. The extended Valdres valley alongside the Begna and Etna rivers to the north became the major center of emigration from the province of Oppland. Historian Terje Mikael Hasle Joranger has assembled the most extensive statistics on especially the Valdres exodus, viewing it in the context of the total emigration from the province. Although there were individual departures early on, regular emigration from the Valdres valley did not start until 1848, when two parties of emigrants left for the American Midwest. According to Hasle Joranger, Valdres accounted for 42.3 percent of all emigrants from Oppland *fylke* between 1851 and 1855, and during the next ten-year period, 1856 to 1865, 43.6 percent; Valdres had during these ten years an annual emigration of 15.6 per thousand people, second only to the district of Sogn. From the mid-1840s until 1865, 13,721 people went overseas from the *fylke*, a number that grew to 21,708 during the following ten years, 1866 to 1875, equal to an annual emigration of 18.1 per thousand of the median population.

The Gudbrandsdalen valley, located on the slopes of the Lågen River, contributed its share of the total. The emigration moved northward in the great valley from the southern communities by Lake Mjøsa, Norway's largest inland lake. The pioneer immigrant Johannes Nordboe left as early as 1832 with his wife and four children from Ringebu; he was then sixty-four years old. At home he had been an outsider, and he did not adapt to the Norwegian settlements, first in Kendall and then in the Fox River Valley, perhaps, as Nordboe himself suggested, because of a deep-seated temperamental difference between the people of eastern and western Norway. It is possible that the Nordboe family, natives of eastern Norway, did not feel at home among the west Norwegian families in the two settlements. In 1838 Nordboe and his family moved to Texas. Nordboe sent many letters home, and even though his relocation did not inspire any immediate followers, his letters and his example did have a stimulating influence on early emigration from eastern Norway. In 1843 he wrote about opportunities in America: "Here a young but poor man can soon become a well-to-do farmer, if he works hard and uses good sense. He can look forward to becoming rich without usury, a difficult task in Norway."

Only in the 1840s, however, was there an increasing emigration; the movement did not reach the northern parts of the valley until the mid-1860s. Many young people in northern Gudbrandsdalen found profitable employment in agriculture and fishing in neighboring Møre og Romsdal *fylke*, which, as stated earlier, prospered and gave work to many. "The spring cod is our America," was one saying, and "Here no one thinks about going to

America." Spring was the traditional departure time for America farers, and attractive opportunities at home during the spring fishing season made emigration less appealing.[14]

Hedmark *fylke*, with the city of Hamar as its administrative center, was another region greatly affected by America fever. Lars Holo from Ringsaker was the pioneer emigrant from the province, leaving in 1839; Nordboe's letters had convinced him to seek a new life in America, where he became Lars Hedemarken. A few more left in the 1840s, and in 1850 as many as 125 emigrated from Ringsaker, while few left from other communities in Hedmark *fylke*. The movement increased thereafter, however; 2,214 left the province between 1856 and 1865. The 11,994 who left between 1866 and 1875 equaled an annual emigration per thousand of 10.0.

The three provinces of Akershus, Østfold, and Vestfold—all bordering the Oslofjord—had only insignificant emigration in the early years of the overseas exodus. A few adventurous individuals left, but the majority of the rural population did not respond to the lure of America, and even though movement increased beginning in 1866, it did not during the following ten years reach even three thousand emigrants from either of the two provinces on opposite sides of the fjord. The populous Akershus *fylke*, in 1865 numbering about 108,000 residents, had during the same decade, 1866–75, a loss of nearly nine thousand citizens, equal to an annual emigration of 8.0 per thousand.

In the first half of the decade of the 1850s, there was a sudden surge from the capital city of Oslo (Christiania). Between 1851 and 1855, 756 left Oslo, which then had a population of about 41,000. Many were craftsmen and artisans. Passport records identify such special occupational skills as cabinetmakers, bricklayers, bookbinders, tailors, shoemakers, and even mates and seamen on sailing ships. Some were office and store clerks; one man listed as "convict" (*tugthusfange*) was obviously starting a new life in America. He represented an element in the overseas movement that is often overlooked. Skilled workers might have decided to emigrate because they felt the threat of cheaper factory-made products, whether imported or manufactured in Norway. They were likely to settle in America's great cities. Only in 1871–75 did urban areas have a greater emigration intensity than the countryside, 7.0 per one thousand to 4.7, although rural Norway retained its lead in absolute numbers.[15]

The Immigrant Population and Norwegian Society

Theodore Blegen depicts the emigrant as a dissenter and a separatist, since "emigration grows out of discontent and restlessness occasioned by burdens of some kind or the hopes of improvement through change, hopefully both." Blegen views the emigrant as a separatist because "his act means a sharp break with familiar conditions," and, Blegen concludes, "he turns his back on his accustomed environment."

Several forces affected Norwegian society in the course of the nineteenth century and gradually produced structural changes. The familiar conditions the emigrants left were altered throughout the emigration era. A high birth rate, described as "the century of large families," and a steadily falling death rate gave Norway one of the highest percentages of population growth in Europe. From a total in 1801 of about 885,000, Norway's population had increased to 1,068,000 in 1825, to 1,340,000 in 1845, and to more than 1,818,000 in 1875, more than doubling in only three-quarters of a century. This great demographic expansion—indeed, an explosive wedge—caused extensive societal transformations. The immense population growth had to be accommodated, either by domestic opportunities or by the more forthright solution of emigration.

Looking at these developments will at least in part answer the basic historical question of why emigration developed when it did and provide some idea of the small and large forces that made an individual decide to emigrate. Sweeping religious revivals, as suggested earlier, were among the strong forces of change, as was political and social dissatisfaction with the prevalent situation.

Norway's population growth was to a high degree rural. According to official statistics, in 1856 as many as 86 percent of the population lived outside the country's small urban centers; in 1865 the rural percentage still stood at 84 percent. In the latter year two-thirds of the population made a living in agriculture, raising cattle, and lumbering, 5.1 percent of the population worked in fisheries, and the portion of the population engaged in industries and mining equaled 15.4 percent. Trade, transportation, and navigation engaged 9.6 percent in 1865. The professions and "nonmaterial work" (*Immaterielt Arbeide*), as the statistics have it, amounted to 3.3 percent. These figures represent Norwegian society at the early advance of modernization. The nineteenth century witnessed great economic changes, in Norway as elsewhere. Industrialization and the modernization of agricultural production arrived late in Norway, but from mid-century, through crisis and setbacks, the industrial sector expanded and a gradual mechanization of farming took place. By 1891, for example, the percentage of the population engaged in farming and allied pursuits had been reduced from 66.6 percent in 1865 to 46.65 percent; industries and mining grew, giving a livelihood to 23.04 percent of the population in the same period. The old export industries, however, remained during the years 1850 to 1890 the large employers of industrial labor and the main earners of foreign exchange. Sima Lieberman states, "Economic growth during this period continued to depend on the export of wood and fish products and on that of shipping services." No heavy industry developed in the period 1850–1900. The creation of new jobs fell far short of the rate required to accommodate the growing population. Labor surpluses were siphoned off through emigration, which continued for a long time to be a conspicuous aspect of the national experience.

Norwegian historian Sverre Steen has described the social circumstances in Norway in the decades before 1850 as "the old society." Much has been made of the fact that Norway never had a feudal system. Instead, the limited and to a great extent poor acreage was owned by a free-holding peasantry, *bønder* (singular, *bonde*). They held their farms under alodial rights, or *odelsrett*, the land passed down from one generation to the next under primogeniture. The main division in peasant society was between landholders and the landless; the latter were cotters or crofters (*husmænd*), renters, laborers, and servants. There existed an insurmountable social distance in the agricultural districts in the flat land in East Norway (Østlandet), in Gudbrandsdalen, and in Trøndelag between the well-to-do farmer with large holdings (*storbonde*) and his cotters; not all landholders were wealthy, but even so the *bønder* were socially above those who lacked land. The same division between landholding and landless farmers existed in West Norway, but the smaller independent farms produced greater social equality.

A structural change occurred in Norwegian society as improved conditions came about in the 1850s, when impressive economic development offered new opportunities for gainful employment. The creation of new jobs did not, however, meet the growing demand. Emigration thus persisted despite the better economic times. During the years 1849–54, Norway lost 21.33 percent of its natural growth, the difference between births and deaths, between natality and mortality, to emigration, and in 1855–60 the percentage sank to 11.48. A process of impoverishment both in the cities and in rural communities caused many people to sink into lower social classes. The comparatively faster growth of the bottom stratum of Norwegian society sharpened class tensions in general. Population pressure was an active factor in the emigration of 1836–65, as well as for the later mass emigration, as were the problems associated with the modernization of agriculture and the resulting crisis beginning in the 1860s. Population growth outstripped available resources; it was especially felt in those regions with the highest rates of emigration. The same inland farming districts saw the greatest loss of citizens to the overseas movement. It continued high in the *fylker* of Oppland, Telemark, and Sogn og Fjordane—especially the local communities mentioned earlier, Sogn, Valdres, and Hallingdal—all with long traditions of emigration and with close ties to Norwegian farming communities in the American Midwest. Emigration also continued from the provinces of Hordaland and Rogaland, where the local districts of Voss, Hardanger, and Ryfylke saw the greatest intensity.

The concepts of "urban field of influence" and "urban barrier" may also be considered when explaining why people emigrated. Swedish scholar Eric De Geer has made a special study of the phenomenon from a Nordic perspective. A city's field of influence defines the surrounding area from which laborers are recruited; many people, for instance, in Akershus *fylke* sought work in nearby Oslo. The considerable distance from the city, on the other hand, of the most affected districts, referred to in sociological terms as the "urban barrier," increased the peasants' anti-urban sentiments. If adequate resources were at hand, this barrier influenced their decision to choose the possibility of making a living in a rural setting overseas over some city or emerging industrial center in Norway.

De Geer points to the fact that, unlike Denmark, where some city or town was always within easy reach of the rural population, Norway—and for that matter Sweden—had a much more dispersed citizenry and a much slower rate of urbanization. The result was accumulation of the explosive population growth in the agricultural districts to a much higher degree than in Denmark. Migration to a middle-sized town was a much more feasible alternative to overseas migration there than in the two other Scandinavian countries and may partly explain the much lower intensity of Danish emigration. The rural populations in Norway and Sweden did not have the same alternatives for internal migration and thus in much greater numbers opted for the New World.[16]

Norwegian society was until the early 1880s ruled by an elite that had established its place in the political structure in the May 17, 1814, constitution, described as the *embetsmann* state—that is, government by an official elite. It had both a political and a social aspect. Academics, especially jurists, constituted the nucleus. The academically trained were the leaders in politics and social life, in art and literature. The Lutheran pastor became the most visible representative of this class in rural parishes. As a social unit, the official class was bound by kinship and acquaintance. Members of this class— the officials and their families—made up only a negligible part of the total population, never more than one percent of Norway's citizens; the system was preserved through inbreeding and self-recruitment. From about 1870 there is evidence that the old social divisions were breaking up and a more modern class structure was emerging. Of particular note, the sons of farmers increasingly entered the ranks of the Lutheran state clergy: in the decade

of the 1860s, eight percent of the theological candidates belonged to the class
of *bønder*, increasing to 20 percent in the following decade. Thus inherited
status became less important and money played a greater role. The new class
of capitalists in commerce and industry became a part of the upper class;
a middle class and a working class came into being. Still, as historian Jostein
Nerbøvik points out, in spite of a more open social system where people
could advance, social differences and discrimination persisted.

The elite's power was challenged early on by the *bønder*, the free-holding
farmers, who constituted the country's second strong social class. Paragraph
fifty in the 1814 constitution accorded voting rights only to officials and
property owners, a system that in the main existed until general voting rights
were granted men in 1898. The free-holding *bønder* challenged the governing elite politically; the farmer opposition established in the 1830s became
a permanent feature. The *bonde* was viewed as the true carrier of Norwegian
nationality, a conviction that gave the democratic ideas of the previous century a national content. The popular movement generated by Hans Nielsen
Hauge and his followers strengthened the *bonde* opposition, especially since
the *embetsmenn* persecuted the movement and earlier had imprisoned Hauge
himself. Many of the *bønder* elected to the Storting were Haugeans or influenced by Haugeanism. In 1832 they won 45 of the 95 seats in the Storting;
the *embetsmenn*'s representation on the other hand was reduced from 40 to 33.
Those now in the minority claimed that the election of the *bønder* was "The
triumph of ignorance and a precursor of barbarity." The law that established
local self-government (*formannskapsloven*), agitated for by the farmer representatives, was sanctioned by Carl Johan, king of Sweden and Norway, on January 14, 1837, the anniversary of the Peace of Kiel. Historian Arne Bergsgård
maintains that "the law was the most important supplement to the constitution ever made." The local government law of 1837 is in general seen by
Norwegian historians as a compromise between the centralizing ideology of
the *embetsmenn* and the *bønder*'s wish for the transfer of power to local bodies.

Changes in Norwegian society were reflected in the composition of the
body of emigrants. The landholding farm households dominated in the early

exodus and had in many cases substantial resources. They might even have means to invest in purchasing farms, usually government land, after their arrival in America. The provincial governor for Lower Telemark reported that for the years 1841–45 each family emigrating from the district left with a sum equal to $2,200 to $4,000, a considerable resource. There was also the wealthy upper-class emigrant Hans Gasmann, who in 1843 sought a better future in America for his thirteen children. The prospects in Norway at the time seemed poor. Gasmann later reported that in America he had achieved what he had hoped for by emigrating: greater happiness for all his children. The decision to seek a better life overseas was for many immigrants far from a flight, but instead was in hope of achieving "a gentler existence," as the provincial governor in Rogaland wrote in 1845. The pre-1850 emigration may thus to a high degree be understood as a stage in upward social mobility.

The lower social classes, cotters and agricultural laborers, were better represented in the emigration beginning in the 1850s. Letters and the increased use of prepaid tickets sent by earlier immigrants encouraged people to emigrate and opened the way west to new social groups. Passage money from America contributed greatly to making the emigrant body more democratic, since it gave mobility to people without resources. The early emigration had a strong family makeup, with the same percentage of children as the Norwegian population in general. The situation lasted until the 1870s, when a shift toward individual departures became apparent. Male emigrants dominated, but in smaller numbers than one might expect. In the years 1866–75, women made up 44 percent of the 119,490 people who left during that decade. In the same period, 28 percent of the male emigrants and 32 percent of the female emigrants were fourteen years old or younger, suggesting the movement's family character.[17]

OF SHIPYARDS AND CREW

Norway's coastal communities had much greater contact with the outside world than did the inland. In fact, the majority of Norwegians lived on the coast. For boys and young men in these communities it was, according to the history of Norwegian shipping, *Norsk sjøfart*, nearly preordained that they would become seamen. Most were fourteen to sixteen years old when they got their first berth as *førstereisgutter*, but some were as young as eleven when they journeyed out. In general young men found employment in the expanding fleet soon after their Lutheran confirmation. Growth in the sailing ship fleet required many new sailors, and as a trade being a seaman gave a passable living. The increase in the percentage of younger seamen is striking. Statistics from the coastal community Hvaler in Østfold *fylke*, a province on the east side of the Oslofjord, show that in 1801 nine percent of seamen from that community were in the fifteen to nineteen age group, while this group in 1865 amounted to 19 percent. In the second half of the century, about

Two *førstereisgutter*, boys who got their first berth at age fourteen or even younger. Following their Lutheran confirmation, young men were considered to be ready for employment. This photo is from about 1917. Conditions did not change much over the decades. *Photo by Ingard Henriksen. Norsk maritimt museum, Oslo, Norway*

half of all sailors from Hvaler were between ages fifteen and twenty-nine, and there were few seamen past the age of forty. Similar changes took place elsewhere as well.

In many coastal communities, being a seaman became a phase in the course of men's lives. A seasoned seaman related the following:

> In 1840 I got my wish to go to seas fulfilled. And at the age of 12 I went onboard the ship *Sophie*, commanded by Captain Larsen from Fredrikstad. It was a fine-looking bark, and on March 12 I was set onboard by my brother as a cabin boy. I did not know anyone onboard, the captain or anyone of the crew, and no one wished me welcome . . . I was attentive and quick . . . I still got a taste of the end of a rope from time to time. It was a part of a good seaman's education.

In the nineteenth century there were few alternative livelihoods, and children followed in the footsteps of their parents. Sailing was a youthful occupation. In the coastal districts and towns there were sailors in nearly every family; few residents did not directly or indirectly have some connection with this particular livelihood. Shipping played an important role in the economy of many coastal communities, particularly in the second half of the nineteenth century, with the great expansion of the Norwegian fleet of sailing ships. Counting Norwegian vessels in near and distant waters, the number of ships amounted in the latter part of the nineteenth century to from four to five thousand, with a combined crew of forty to fifty thousand men. The size of the crew depended on the vessel's tonnage as well as on how it was rigged and equipped. The two-masted brig *Odin*, which departed from Bergen on April 24 and landed in Quebec on July 2, 1854, belonged to the medium-sized category; brigs had, as recorded for the fleet in Bergen, an average tonnage of 217 and a crew of about seven men. The three-masted bark *Fædre Minde*, introduced earlier, transported emigrants from Oslo to Quebec the same year; barks were larger than brigs and had an average tonnage of 572 and an approximate crew of thirteen men.

Gøthe Gøthesen paints a vivid portrait of "seamen's lives in the era of sailing ships." Social differences were obvious at sea. The skipper or captain was at the top of the social ladder, and at the bottom, as suggested by the quote above, stood the *førstereisgutt*, the young boy making his first voyage, whether he was a cook or a cabin boy or a deck boy. A distinct order of rank from top to bottom was carried out in nearly all circumstances, from living quarters to meals, but not least in the division of labor. The position of the captain is emblematic. Gøthesen quotes a young boy on his first voyage on the bark *Valkyrien:* "The captain spoke as little as possible with us. On board he was king by the grace of God and Mrs. Thorsen [the shipowner's widow], and was seen as a supernatural being."

Bark "Hebe" - 1886

The crew on the bark *Hebe* of Stavanger in 1886. The man with the cane and derby hat is Captain Knud Olsen. The boy sitting in front is Georg Kerstin Thorsen, age fifteen. Later he became a captain. *Photographer unknown. Stavanger maritime museum, Stavanger, Norway*

Cabins and bunks were distributed according to rank and social status; a specific area of the ship before the main mast was reserved for the officers and was taboo for the crew. The captain had great leeway to exercise discipline. The maritime law of 1860 accorded the captain the same authority over his crew as "a master of a household over his servants." Only in 1893 did the law clearly prohibit "corporal punishment."

Besides the captain, the officers included the navigator, his duty to determine position and navigate the ship across the ocean. Knowledge of navigation by a ship's officers did not, however, become a requirement before Norway's first navigation law, which was enacted only in 1840, when men had to pass a test in order to sail as captains or mates. Overseas voyages made the requirement essential; instruction in navigation had also been given earlier in one form or other. The first mate was the second in command and likely the officer who had most to do on board. In addition to being the commanding officer on the port watch, he was the actual assigner of work, charged with seeing that the captain's orders were followed. He was also responsible for the ship's seaworthiness, making sure that rigging, lifeboats, and other rescue equipment, as well as the anchor gear, were in working condition. Most Norwegian ships generally had a second mate who as a rule—though not always—was a trained navigator. The reason might be, as Gøthesen suggests, that the captain himself might make the rounds and thereby save the expense of a trained navigator.

A core of able and self-confident seamen who knew what to do in critical situations was essential on the sailing ships. A competent seaman (*matros*) was thus highly regarded by both his fellows and the officers. A boy would likely serve from two to three or four years to become an able-bodied seaman. The ordinary seaman (*lettmatros*) and the naval rank *jungmann* were a step above the *førstereisgutt*. Then there were the cook and the steward. The cook was regularly a boy on his first voyage with little or no experience in preparing food. Toward the end of the 1800s, he was replaced with the steward, especially on long voyages; the steward was a grown man, usually with some insight into cooking. The change improved standards and provided better meals.

Finally, there were the carpenter (*tømmermann*) and sailmaker. A carpenter's foremost responsibility revolved around maintenance, repairs, and possible renovations on board. Gøthesen says, "He must also see to it that the water remained where it belonged—on the outside of the vessel." It was thus his charge to caulk the deck, sides, and prow, to batten down the hatches, and, not the least, to see to it that the pumps were in good working condition.

The bark was the most common vessel under sail in the Norwegian merchant fleet. A bark carried about twenty-two sails. Every sail had to be kept up and looked over. This was, as Gøthesen points out, especially challenging

The crew on board the full-rigged *Manx King*, built in 1884. The photo was taken in Buenos Aires, Argentina. *Photo by Ingard Henriksen. Norsk maritimt museum, Oslo, Norway*

in areas with harsh weather conditions, where sails required much patching and maintenance. A fully trained sailmaker was regarded highly. The ships sailing in distant waters were most likely to hire a man who had mastered his trade; all sailing ships, however, had people on board who could tend to the sails, frequently a sailor who had gained knowledge while under way.[18]

Shipbuilding was done in shipyards spread along Norway's long coastline from Trøndelag and south; farther north, shipyards were operated mainly for repair and maintenance, though sailing ships were on occasion built there. Until 1880 a substantial number of Norwegian ships were built in Norway; the construction of wooden ships culminated in 1875 when close to two hundred vessels, taking into account all ships regardless of tonnage, were built.

In a long chapter titled "Our Seafaring Cities," Nils Vigeland systematically treats some twenty-five or more coastal towns, their engagement in the construction of sailing ships, and their commercial activity based on shipping, beginning with Trondheim and concluding with the settlements in Østfold *fylke*. People harbored great faith in the commercial returns of sailing ships, and without such strong belief, Vigeland maintains, a country like Norway, poor in capital, would never have been able to undertake the heavy work required to build up the fleet. The one-sided disposition in economic life during the sailing ship era allowed the coastal towns to a high degree to feel the shifting economic conditions in Europe. They experienced one crisis after another, and the economic downturn in 1848 severely affected many coastal communities. But, Vigeland reports, "right afterwards came the shipping on Canada and free trade and created a golden age."

Emigration from the provinces Vest- and Aust-Agder on Norway's south coast, defined as Sørlandet, may illustrate the effect of the growing commercial activity during the era of the sailing ships. A few hundred people had emigrated from Sørlandet before 1850; among these was Johan R. Reiersen, mentioned earlier, who in 1843 set out for America as an agent for a group of people who wanted to emigrate. As editor of the reform newspaper *Christiansandsposten*, published in Kristiansand, Vest-Agder, he spoke enthusiastically about America and encouraged emigration. Upon his return to

Norway in 1844, he published his guidebook to the United States and Texas. He maintained that Texas, with its good climate and easy access to land, was the best place for a Norwegian colony. In 1845 Reiersen himself moved permanently to Texas with his family and a few other emigrants as an advance party; others moved there from southern Norway in the following years. But Reiersen's plan of a large permanent Norwegian colony in Henderson County, near present-day Brownsboro, in northern Texas, or "New Normandy," the name he proudly chose, was not realized.

Beginning in the 1850s, emigration from the two Agder *fylker* declined. From then on shipbuilding and shipping expanded rapidly; districts within the provinces had large surpluses of people moving to the area. The sailing ship traffic flourished, as did shipbuilding. Indeed, the coastal region of all of Sørlandet, with its "white cities and all their attractive clusters of houses in sheltered harbors," was in economic terms a thriving part of the country. Not until toward the end of the nineteenth century, when sailing ships were displaced by steamships, did emigration to America gain strength in the two Agder provinces. It is another example of how the growth of local livelihoods counteracted emigration.

Not all ships sailing under the Norwegian flag were built in Norway, and some shipowners found it convenient to acquire a vessel from abroad that could immediately be put into service. Many of these ships were of older tonnage. Purchased foreign ships came especially to East Norway. Bergen, among other cities on the west and south coast, invested in building ships, though those built outside Norway were also purchased, but not in large numbers. In 1869, for instance, forty of 277 ships in Norway's merchant fleet were purchased from abroad, striking evidence of the large share of ships built at home. Along the coast of Sørlandet, it was claimed, one could in every little fjord see a ship on the bedding or a keel being laid. Of course, coastal towns farther east and along the Oslofjord also housed shipyards in effective operation.

Details of the bedding operations along the coast will be discussed broadly here. The dominant form of shipping firms during the sailing ships era was

based on joint ownership, *partrederi*, partnership, which meant, as Helge
Nordvik writes, "that financial resources could be mobilized from a surpris-
ingly large part of the population." Before 1850 the group of owners was
generally small, consisting of family, neighbors, and friends, but after the
middle of the century the number of part owners increased. Shipping firms
or partnerships might also be owned by a small group of individual mer-
chants. Many merchant houses continued to be active in shipping after 1850.
It might even happen that a ship was owned by the entire crew. In addition
to the captain, as reported in 1861–65 from Vest-Agder *fylke*, the farmers
who delivered material for shipbuilding became part owners. *Norsk sjøfart*
maintains that people might pawn both house and land in order to acquire
a part in a ship. There were, according to the same source, as many part–
shipping firms as there were ships. Shipping companies existed in both
town and country on the coast. In 1875 3,915 sailing ships belonged in cities
and 3,008 were from rural districts. The majority of part owners lived in the
countryside.

In 1860 the country's largest maritime cities were in Østlandet and Sørlandet. Arendal had the largest fleet, thereafter Tønsberg, then Drammen,
then Oslo. In Vestlandet, Stavanger was listed as having the fifth-largest fleet
and Bergen had sixth place. In terms of value and efficiency, the merchant
fleet in Bergen was well equipped to take advantage of the good times in
international shipping in the 1860s and 1870s; it saw strong growth as a
maritime town, in terms of tonnage by 1894 second only to Oslo. The growth
in shipping in Norway after 1850 was made possible by capital accumulated
in the timber trade from southern coastal towns, the herring trade from
Stavanger, and the saltfish and stockfish trade from Bergen.

A crucial element, as Nordvik reminds us, in the successful expansion of
the Norwegian shipping industry during the period 1850–80 was the close
cooperation between shipowners and shipbuilders. Ships were built along
the entire coast, and for five years, 1851–55, the number of vessels built in the
kingdom stood at 964, response to an increased demand for tonnage from
the Crimean War and the overseas trade to Canada. Norwegian shipowners

This banner, painted by J. F. Løsting, shows the launching of the bark
Valkyrien in 1868 at the Bradbenken shipyard in Bergen, Norway. *Stiftelsen
Bergens sjøfartsmuseum, Bergen, Norway*

were able to offer lower rates, which expanded the Norwegian fleet as well.
In order to reduce operating costs, the ships had to be built cheaply and the
crew had to be as small as possible; wages were also lower than, for example,
on American ships. The endeavor to operate cheaply influenced the ships'
rigging as well. The schooner was consequently preferred to the brig and the
bark to the full-rigged ship.

   Bergen was the first shipping city in Norway to have outstanding professional designers, and for that reason its fleet held a unique position in regard
to quality. The shipyard Georgenes, founded by Georg Vedeler and Georg
Brunchorst, had its greatest success under the leadership of Annanias Dekke.

His life and experience provide insight into his trade as a shipwright. He began working for the shipyard at the age of sixteen. At age twenty, he studied shipbuilding and design in Sweden, England, Scotland, and the United States. Dekke saw the launching of clippers in cities such as Baltimore, Boston, and New York. The greatest progress in shipbuilding at midcentury was made in the United States, centering on the clipper, noted for its speed and leaving all other sailing ships behind. Donald McKay, born in Nova Scotia, became the best-known clipper builder of his time.

Dekke worked under McKay and returned to Bergen with glowing recommendations. In 1853 he purchased half of Georgenes shipyard, which became Brunchorst and Dekke. Dekke's masterwork was the high-speed frigate *Hebe*, launched in 1856. With its clipper bow, elegant lines, and thirty different sails, it gave, as Vigeland explains, an impression of being more a yacht than a merchant ship. The *Hebe* engaged in emigrant traffic to North America, in 1856 making its first crossing to Quebec from Bergen in four weeks. In Quebec it created a great stir and was downright admired. Dekke was not the only ship designer in Bergen who had learned the trade in America, but because his designs—"Dekke's creations," as they were called—were distributed to other shipyards, he became known in all Nordic countries.

The Norwegian sailing ship had its most glorious period from the end of the 1860s into the 1870s, before steamships asserted themselves in the competition for emigrant transport. The transition to steam is a topic in the following chapter. In terms of tonnage, the sailing ships in the Norwegian merchant fleet reached their culmination as late as 1891. Norway boasted a proud, though minute, sailing ship fleet even after World War I. Before the next global conflict, however, a merchant fleet of sailing ships belonged to the past.[19]

chapter 3

The Canadian Epoch

*T*he term *epoch* denotes a period in history marked by notable events. In terms of Canadian immigration, this chapter will tell the distinctive stories of the recruitment of Norwegian emigrants by Canadian authorities, the crossing from Norway to Quebec Province, the first encounter with the new environment, and the establishment of Norwegian colonies and their shifting fortunes.

This history includes the impact of emigrant agents in recruiting passengers and settlers, the arrival at Grosse Île and ports of entry, the unsuccessful efforts of Canadian authorities to retain more Norwegian settlers, and the failure of the Gaspé colony. Desertion by crew members upon landing in Canadian port cities was clearly a factor in Norwegian emigration; sailortowns were also places where seamen were exploited and shanghaied. The Atlantic crossing and the situation on board the passenger vessels will be given a full account. The fate of the many indigent emigrants stranded in Quebec is a part of the story, as is the history of the transition from sail to steam passenger ships.

Outward Bound

Ships carrying emigrants to Quebec departed from all coastal cities, but Bergen and Oslo in time became the most important gateways. Some also made it across in small groups from their home tracts. For the approximately

60,000 emigrants who left for North America between 1851 and 1865, Oslo and Bergen dominated as departure points, with 29 percent boarding a ship in Bergen and six percent leaving indirectly for another European port from Oslo and 22 percent directly to North America, for a total of about 33,000 emigrants, or 56 percent.

Oslo's role as Norway's capital city intensified in the nineteenth century as manifested by the construction of important buildings. Akershus Castle and Fortress from the 1300s, located on the Oslofjord, is a majestic and visible reminder of the city's medieval status. The Royal Palace, home to the present Norwegian monarch, was built in the first half of the nineteenth century and was completed in 1848 as the residence of the King of Sweden and Norway when he paid a visit to the Norwegian capital. Oslo, or Christiania, had at mid-century a population of about 42,000. In 1852 the main street, connecting the royal palace with the rest of the city, was named Karl Johan in honor

The medieval Akershus Castle and Fortress seen from the northwest in the 1860s. *Photo by Adolf Christian Moestue. Oslo museum, Oslo, Norway*

of the recently deceased king. His equestrian statue in front of the palace was erected in 1875. Located along Karl Johan are the university buildings finished in 1853; a little farther down the street is the parliamentary building, housing the Norwegian Storting or parliament, dating from 1866. To later generations, these government structures symbolize *embetsmannsstaten*—government by the elite. During the emigration season the capital became a port city humming with ships, suppliers, agents, and emigrants.

Bergen, known as the city of seven mountains, was Norway's largest urban area until 1830, when it was surpassed by the capital, Oslo. At mid-century it housed about 25,000 citizens. Emigrants coming from its upland or more distant regions to secure voyage to North America entered a place with a long history; from the end of the thirteenth century it was a bureau city of the Hanseatic League, a commercial and defensive confederation of merchant guilds and their market towns that dominated trade along the coast of

A photo taken of the royal palace in Christiania (Oslo) from the Trinity Lutheran Church in the 1860s. *Photo by Adolf Christian Moestue. Oslo museum, Oslo, Norway*

northern Europe. The remaining medieval wharves referred to as Bryggen—
also known as Tyskebryggen, the German Wharf, with its Hanseatic wooden
commercial buildings—are reminders of the international contacts the city
enjoyed. A foreign strain was visible in its population through migration
from northern Germany, the Netherlands, and Scotland. During the decade
1856 to 1866, Bergen was the largest emigrant shipping port in the country.
The shipowners in Bergen, however, engaged increasingly in the expanding
trade with the United States and had less interest in the combined emigrant
and timber trade with Canada. The emigrant traffic directly from Norway to
Quebec, as a consequence, was dominated by vessels from eastern provinces
from the 1860s until 1874, when the last passenger sailing ship left Norway.

Other seaports, save for Trondheim, with 19,000 inhabitants in 1855, were
considerably smaller, the largest being Stavanger, with a population in 1855
of about 12,000. The main seaports are listed in a sequence showing the volume of emigrants. Drammen, in the province of Buskerud and with fewer
than 10,000 citizens at mid-century, accounted for 11 percent of departures;
the cities in Telemark *fylke*, among these the seaport cities of Skien, Porsgrunn,
and Kragerø, had 16 percent of all departing emigrants during these same
years; cities in Aust-Agder *fylke*, with the port cities of Risør, Arendal, and
Grimstad, three percent; the cities in Rogaland *fylke*, mainly Stavanger, nine
percent, and Trondheim, indirectly and directly combined, two percent.
Though fewer emigrated from Vest-Agder, Kristiansand, the largest city in the
two Agder provinces, with a population of about 9,500 in 1855, was nevertheless an important shipping outlet. These were the main ports of departure
during the most decisive years—1851 to 1865—when Quebec was the destination for the great majority, in fact 87 percent, of all Norwegian emigrants.

The port cities were bustling places. During the emigration season, beginning in early April, peasants dressed in homespun clothes and with supplies
of food and equipment filled the streets as they waited to get passage to
America. The following, from a long article in *Skilling-Magazin* titled "Onboard
an Emigrant Ship" and describing the voyage of a sailing ship from its start
in Oslo to its landing in Quebec, offers a vivid view:

The port of Bergen in the 1860s. *Courtesy of Rolf Svellingen*

The Christiania (Oslo) harbor with sailing ships, as seen from the Ekeberg heights in 1865. *Photo by Jens Peter Broch. Oslo museum, Oslo, Norway*

If on a day in the month of April one should take a walk down to the customs house on the new docks in Christiania [Oslo], one would most likely catch sight of well-dressed *bonde* families, men, women, and children, waiting to be put onboard a ship. They have arrived with their luggage, a diverse collection of boxes and chests. One reads: Paul Larsen, Milwaukee, Wisconsin, North America; Ole Andersen, Chicago, Illinois, North America; Peder Gulbrandsen, Madison, Wisconsin, North America; Olivia Eriksdatter Nordreie, Iowa, Minnesota, and a great number of other names and addresses. There are sacks of potatoes, kettles and pans, fire pokers, stools, *tiner* [bentwood oval boxes], sacks of bread, beer and brandy kegs, herring quarters, cloth covered cured meat, children's buggies, mattresses, and straw quilts all mixed up in a chaos. All of it to be taken onboard.

The sailing ships did not have posted times of departure, as these were contingent on a sufficient number of passengers having acquired passage. A standard advertisement was printed in *Christiania-Posten* on February 5, 1853: "In the course of the month of April, the high speed and well suited for passenger traffic ship *Tegnér*, commanded by Captain Falck, will depart for Quebec with passengers, provided that a sufficient number sign up . . . As soon as a certain number of passengers are signed up, the departure date will be determined." The announcement was signed by ship broker Winge, who likely was a part owner in *Tegnér*.

Shipowners and captains did not simply make their service known through the press but took an active part in recruiting passengers. It might take time to enlist a sufficient number of passengers, and as a consequence people intending to emigrate might linger in a port city for days or weeks before the ship was ready to set sail. The different shipowners with traffic to New York and Quebec competed for passengers. Emigration agents, and even some skippers of emigrant ships, visited rural districts in order to enroll emigrants; they portrayed America in the most favorable terms in order to convince people to book passage. As early as the 1840s, the Bergen journal *Bergens Stiftstidende* sharply condemned the practice. The emigration agents who entered the trade were actually asked only to sign contracts with people who already had decided to emigrate, but in order to fill the ship they did their best to convince people to leave. In a sense they reinforced the message of the positive America letters; the latter were of course more credible for the local population. The emigration agents distributed their message where many people were gathered: on the church green after a Sunday service, at marketplaces, and even at country weddings—in other words, in circumstances where "many were in a frame of mind where ordinary inhibitions and hesitations disappeared." The question remains, however, whether many were convinced to emigrate who already were not considering doing just that. The activities of the early emigration agents, until the 1860s, appeared incidental and were not organized.[1]

Bekjendtgjørelse

angaaende Befordring af

Emigranter til Quebek eller Montreal

med Seilskibe.

Flere første Classes udmærket gode Seilskibe ville blive expederede herfra til Quebek eller Montreal med Passagerer i anstundende April og Mai Maaned.

Fragten til Quebek er 12 Spd. for vorne Personer over 14 Aar.

             9 — „ halvvorne do. mellem 10 og 14 Aar.

             6 — „ Børn — 1 og 10 Aar.

             Børn under 1 Aar betale ingen Fragt.

Desuden betales af Enhver, som er over 1 Aar, 1 Spd. i Landgangspenge eller amerikansk Kopskat.

Til Montreal bliver Fragten 1 Spd. mere pro Person.

Passagererne erholde paa Reisen frit Vand, Lys, Brænde, Salt og Medicin samt en honet og venlig Behandling af Skibets Fører og Mandskab.

Indskrivningspenge er 10 a 12 Spd. for Familier, ifølge Størrelsen, og 5 Spd. for løse Personer.

Ved Familie forstaaes kun Mand, Kone og Børn af samme Husstand, Tjenere betragtes som løse Personer.

Noiagtig Alder, fulde Navn samt Gaardsnavn og Præstegjeld maa tydelig opgives.

Indskrivning bør ske saa tidlig som muligt paa Foraaret, helst i Januar og Februar.

Passagererne har som sædvanlig selv at bekoste sig hertil og ombord i Skibet, og skal Contoret paa Forlangende være dem behjelpelig med at betinge Dampskibs-Befordring hertil m. v.

Lovbefalet Contract vil strax ved Passagerernes Ankomst hertil blive enhver især overleveret, før at kunne blive paategnet af Politimesteren.

Enhver Passager maa være forsynet med lovbefalet Proviant for 12 Uger, ligesaa og med nødvendige Midler til Reisens Fortsættelse fra Landingsstedet til Bestemmelsesstedet i Amerika, og som mindst maa være 10 Spd. pr. voxen Person, 5 Spd. for Børn, der bliver at deponere hos Captainen før Afreisen herfra.

Uden at Indskrivningspenge ere erlagte, betragtes Ingen som indskreven Passager.

Nærmere Underretning erholdes ved at henvende sig til det autoriserede Emigrantbefordringscontor herfteds, som under Politimesterens Controll vil drage al fornøden Omsorg for Udvandrende.

Skrivelser i bcorte Anledning adresseres til

Bergen i December 1860.

Emigrantbefordringscontoret.

EMIGRATION AGENTS

Whether or not the activities of the agents actually increased the total emigration—making the emigration wave artificially high, for example—remains a question debated among historians. The popular contemporary opinion appeared to support the view that agents had great influence on individual decisions and were frequently criticized. In 1866 *Morgenbladet* complained about the agent system and the foreign steamship companies that sent their "emissaries around the country in order to capture souls." The result according to the newspaper was that "the thoughtless, uninformed, and destitute part of our population . . . is enticed to emigrate by false accounts from America of easy access to an extraordinary large earnings for their labor."

Compared to the social and economic forces that inspired emigration, it is evident that the spread of information, the transportation system, and emigration agents of all kinds played a secondary role. Yet it is hardly reasonable to completely dismiss the influence of the emigration agents and the undertakings they represented. Their decisive role as recruiters in the north Norwegian emigration has been mentioned. Accessible and reliable information provided by people who had the community's trust must have had some effect elsewhere in Norway as well, and the fact that the journey could be planned and arranged from the home community to the final destination in North America must have encouraged at least some vacillating and undecided individuals to emigrate. Even so, crediting agents' activity with a decisive impact on the size of the emigrant body from year to year is at best speculative. The so-called Yankee system might have been a more effective propaganda apparatus. In the Yankee system, Norwegian Americans functioned as agents for steamship lines and other economic interests; the visiting Norwegian American offered, as advertised, "a good opportunity and company for emigrants." The visitor served as guide and advisor on the Atlantic crossing.

The system as organized by different ship companies consciously strove to communicate directly with urban and rural communities throughout Norway. In 1867 Oslo, by then the most significant emigration port, had as many as ten general agencies for as many steamship companies. The British Allan

Shipping Line (Montreal Ocean Steamship Company), represented in Oslo by A. Sharpe, in the early steamship period led in Norwegian emigration. Under the general agency in 1873 there were 305 subagents, a number that in the following years rose to 619, spread throughout the land from Vardø in the north to Kristiansand in the south, frequently with more than one subagent in the most important emigration districts. An agent paid on a commission basis might do well and secure a good income, even though beginning in the 1850s an increasing number of emigrants received prepaid tickets from America.

The Allan Line advertised itself in Norway as the "only line to Canada," with departures from Glasgow and Liverpool and landings in Halifax, Quebec, and Montreal. The line continued to announce that its route was "considerably shorter than to New York and Boston." From 1869 Norwegian emigrants booked on one of the Allan Line's transatlantic steamers could make it across to Britain on one of its steamships operated from Norwegian ports such as Trondheim to Hull. The Norwegian Emigration Society (*Det norske Udvandringsselskab*) in Oslo offered transportation on sailing ships directly to Quebec until the society was dissolved in 1873. The Stavanger shipping company J. A. Køhler continued as well to offer passenger transportation to Quebec, in 1861 announcing that its ship *Hebe* would "be ready for departure April 25." In Trondheim ship broker Wm. Brown also persisted in announcing "Shipping Opportunity to America"; as stated above, departures on sailing ships were contingent on collecting a sufficient number of passengers, as seen in the notice from 1862: "Captain J. H. Koen, commanding the brig *Brødrene*, well known to emigrants, has firmly decided to leave from here for Gaspé and Quebec the first days of May with emigrants. More detailed information about the notation may be had from Mr. J. Jessen Koen or the undersigned. Wm. Brown."[2]

Emigrated Norwegians were recruited as agents. Two early examples in this category were John Holfeldt and Elias Stangeland, who represented competing economic interests; a strife developed between them and is well documented in the Norwegian and Norwegian American press. They confronted each other in New York and later in Quebec. Holfeldt arrived in New York from Norway in 1846 and became an emigration agent; he assisted Scandinavian immigrants in arranging transportation inland and thereby protected them against exploitation by "runners." Stangeland was an emigrant from Avaldsnes on the island of Karmøy and was a pioneer settler at Muskego, Wisconsin, in 1848. In April 1852, the newspaper *Emigranten,* frequently the voice of the Norwegian Synod, carried an announcement signed by Synod pastors stating that "at our request, two reliable, honest, and Christian-minded men, namely Aslak Olnæs from Koshkonong and Elias Stangeland from Muskego, have taken it upon themselves to go to New York this summer to assist arriving Norwegian immigrants secure contracts with reliable companies for transportation inland and to serve as interpreters."

Holfeldt and Stangeland had similar responsibilities. But that same year Holfeldt was hired by famed Norwegian violinist Ole Bull as an agent for his grand plans for a Norwegian colony, Oleana, in Potter County, Pennsylvania. Stangeland vigorously campaigned against Bull's colony, promoting instead settlement in the Middle West, especially Wisconsin. On March 17, 1853, *Emigranten* carried a letter dated in Kongsberg, Norway, from two "returned countrymen" in support of Stangeland and opposing Holfeldt; they did not want their countrymen "to fall into the clutches of Ole Bull's agents." Holfeldt himself resigned as agent for the failed Bull colony; he announced in *Emigranten* on March 25, 1853, that he could no longer advise emigrants to move to Oleana.

Holfeldt thereafter moved to Quebec as transportation agent. He advertised his services in *Emigranten:* "Everyone who next summer wishes to help their relatives to come over here from Norway, is hereby informed that I after request have arranged it so that I can provide money orders that will be accepted for transportation on ships that depart for Quebec from Christiania [Oslo], Skien, Stavanger, and Bergen." Holfeldt took advantage of a great increase in the sale of "prepaid tickets" and the fact that nearly all Norwegian emigrants to North America at the time entered through the Canadian gateway.

Stangeland had gone to Norway the fall of 1852 as an agent of the American forwarding company Maxwell and Patten, headquartered in Buffalo. The company would transport Norwegian emigrants to the Midwest from Quebec and New York. Stangeland traveled around Norway giving speeches about America. In the spring of 1853 he published the manual *Nogle veiledende Vink for norske Udvandrere til Amerika* (Some Guiding Suggestions for Norwegian Emigrants to America). In it he gives solid advice on practical problems associated with the journey and urges the use of Norwegian sailing vessels to Quebec and, to be sure, the Maxwell and Patten forwarding company to Wisconsin. Stangeland took care not to encourage people to emigrate and was well received by the *bonde* politician Ole Gabriel Ueland and pastors in the Church of Norway. In a letter dated March 29, 1853, and printed in *Christiania-Posten*, Ueland endorsed Stangeland's plan, which was "to offer the emigrants transportation from the coast to the western states," which Ueland found to be reasonable and "would secure the emigrants against the unjust treatment and swindle which they so often are exposed to."

Not everyone agreed. Stangeland soon found himself under attack, his actions criticized in the newspaper *Emigranten* and reprinted in newspapers in Norway. These attacks began as early as December 26, 1852, in an article which referred to Stangeland as "a so-called interpreter" who went home to Norway to entice people to emigrate. In a long piece printed in *Emigranten* on April 19, 1853, Pastor A. C. Preus of the Norwegian Synod accused Stangeland of misusing his and other midwestern ministers' earlier endorsement in order to gain acceptance in Norway, denounced his enterprise as humbug, attacked the entire system of runners and agents, and advised emigrants to deal directly with Norwegian ship captains and ask them to arrange passage from New York and Quebec to the Midwest. There were complaints from passengers and even documented cases where emigrants in transit had been unjustly treated by Maxwell and Patten. These complaints damaged Stangeland's reputation.

One interpretation of the Synod pastors' motives might be their concern for the emigrants' welfare, but the controversy appears to be driven just as much by personal antagonism. Maxwell and Patten submitted a defense to *Emigranten*'s editor together with a letter from Stangeland to the company; these were translated into Norwegian and printed in *Emigranten* in July 1853. Maxwell and Patten assured readers that the company had the emigrants' welfare constantly in mind and announced that it had "engaged a good man, a Mr. Christian Wold, Norwegian and a subscriber to your newspaper; he is now in Quebec and will there attend to the emigrants' interests." No more is known about Wold, but his appointment may be seen as a favorable measure by the forwarding company.

In his letter to Maxwell and Patten from Norway, Stangeland gives an account of the number of passengers he has made contracts with to New York and Quebec; he also informs his employers that he has engaged sub-agents in Stavanger and Bergen who were "smart fellows, it is better you believe." *Emigranten*'s editor was not able to translate the quoted statement into Norwegian. Stangeland implores "Dear Friends!" as he calls Maxwell and Patten, to "instruct your agents in Quebec and New York to keep a sharp watch on the emigrants and the runners." There is no recorded evidence of fraud by Stangeland, save perhaps for his claim to be endorsed by the ministers. When he returned to Wisconsin, he started publication of a newspaper he titled *Den Norske Amerikaner* (The Norwegian American); the purpose was to create an outlet to defend himself against personal attacks from the Synod pastors' secular *Emigranten*. The newspaper became a platform to express antipathy against the pastors, yielding a controversy that lasted for some time.

In its June 16, 1854, issue *Emigranten* announced Stangeland's appointment as agent for the state of Wisconsin, stationed at Quebec to influence incoming Norwegian immigrants to settle in that state. His activities will be considered further in chapter four. In Quebec he again encountered his competitor in the transportation of Norwegian emigrants, John Holfeldt, and the two along with their supporters engaged in bitter newspaper polemics in the Norwegian American press. There was personal animosity, but their captious exchanges illustrated as well the strong competitive spirit among agents and the companies they served.

Canadian authorities eagerly sought immigrants, and they appointed agents to promote immigration to and settlement in Canada. This particular class of agents represented Canadian economic and social considerations. Norwegian immigrants were among the favored, described by A. C. Buchanan, Quebec's chief emigration agent, as "valuable settlers," and he worked "to secure large numbers of Norwegians." Buchanan, given his major presence as an emigration agent, deserves a full introduction. He was born in County Tyrone, Northern Ireland, in 1808; in 1816 his father was appointed British consul in New York and brought the family to the United States. In 1825 Buchanan came to Montreal, Canada, and there became a shipping merchant and gained considerable knowledge of and interest in emigration. His uncle, also named A. C. Buchanan, was the British agent for emigration at Quebec from 1828 until 1838. Due to his uncle's poor health, the younger Buchanan became his assistant, and in 1835 he took charge of the office; on July 1, 1838, the British government appointed him chief emigration agent.

Buchanan's responsibilities included enforcing the new regulations and insuring that the requirements of the recently passed Passenger Act were observed, prosecuting masters for breach of the act, and assisting new arrivals in finding work or making their way to settlements in the interior. Vessels were to be inspected before departure and again upon arrival in Canada. Britain passed a number of passenger acts—1835, 1842, 1847—to strengthen regulations intended to ensure emigrants' welfare and safety. The 1842 act was a comprehensive emigrant protection law to control overcrowding, accord each passenger a specific deck space, and establish minimum food and water provisions. By 1845 emigrants could, according to the act, require shipowners to provide them with supplies and lodging if their departure was delayed, and the ship's captain was required to ensure that steerage quarters were kept clean. British middle-class moralism was reflected in the act of 1847; to maintain propriety between the sexes, it required masters to have separate quarters for single women and men. Norwegian ships carrying passengers and the emigrants themselves, along with other nationalities, as historian Oliver MacDonagh states, became subjects of "the new regulations and growing bureaucracies related to emigration and colonization," which, he maintains, "inadvertently laid the groundwork of a modern British state." Laws passed in Norway intending to protect emigrants during their voyage across the Atlantic will be considered in the following section.

By the 1860s, Buchanan ceased to have the status of an imperial official and became a Canadian civil servant; the evolution was brought about by the achievement of responsible government in Canada. It was a long process that began in 1848 when Buchanan submitted his reports to the executive council of the Province of Canada before transmission to London; in the following years as chief emigration agent Buchanan was required to present his reports to the legislative assembly. In 1852 the Canadian government established a bureau of agriculture, which had immigration as one of its charges; in 1855 Canada assumed responsibility for the total cost of immigration services within its province. Then, in 1861, after the department of agriculture and statistics was established, Buchanan's reports were included in those of the Canadian minister of agriculture. These developments led up to confederation and the creation of the Dominion of Canada in 1867.

Buchanan's experience with immigration in Canada and his knowledge of conditions in Europe led him in 1852 to advocate sending Canadian emigration agents to the Continent. However, the first one was not sent until 1859, when Anthony Brewden Hawke became emigration agent in England. The Canadian government most consistently sought to attract farmers with capital, farm laborers, and female domestic servants. Buchanan's biography includes the following assessment of his work: "Buchanan's chief contributions to Canada's development were his careful administration of the immigration agency in Quebec and his consistent support for a Canadian presence overseas particularly in the form of emigration agencies."

In his report for 1860 (published in 1861), Buchanan outlines the work done. He maintained, as seen in later reports, harmonious relations with the agents he sent to Europe. German and Norwegian arrivals constituted for some time the major percentage of emigrants with no knowledge of either English or French, the two common languages in the province. In the 1861 report, Buchanan identifies Helge Haugan and Christopher Closter as the two Norwegian agents. Their specific roles and achievements as immigration agents will be dealt with more fully in later sections. Buchanan begins his 1860 report by describing how thousands of a valuable pamphlet on Canada and "her vast resources have been distributed, not only in Great Britain and Ireland, but in Prussia, Germany, Norway, and France, having been translated into French, German, and Norwegian." William Wagner, of Prussian birth and "intimately acquainted with the Province of Canada, from several years residence . . . was sent to Prussia and Germany, and fully supplied with many hundreds of pamphlets, translated into the German language, and accompanied with large and accurate maps of the Province." Samples of excellent wheat were sent to Germany for public exhibition. Wagner reported that he expected a large German emigration to Canada during the coming season.

The minister of agriculture had paid similar attention to secure the immigration of large numbers of Norwegians. Buchanan reported the following testimonial: "A Mr. Helge Haugan, a very intelligent Norwegian, who had been settled in the township of Bury, Lower Canada, for some time, and was acquainted with the soil, climate, and resources of the Province, was upon his leaving for Norway, entrusted with a number of maps and pamphlets in the Norwegian language, for distribution, and was employed to travel to the most important sea-ports and other Towns in Norway to diffuse a knowledge of Canada."

Haugan was born in Drammen, where according to information from the town's public library he worked as a carriage maker before emigrating. No obituary has been uncovered. A letter included in Buchanan's report tells of Haugan's activities after his return to Norway in March 1860; he relates that he had opened an emigration office in Christiania (Oslo) and a sub-agency in Trondheim for the northern part of Norway and made contacts in the Lofoten islands and in the town of Vadsø in eastern Finnmark *fylke.* His efforts were, however, met with distrust both in Oslo and Trondheim, a situation Orm Øverland attributes to the prejudice of a class-conscious Norway against an emigrated craftsman who could claim no established contacts with people of influence in society. The success Haugan achieved as an agent was mainly tied to his undertakings in Trondheim and northward. Haugan believed a great number of emigrants would leave Norway the following spring "and settle the land district by the Ottawa River." The Ottawa country in Upper Canada, after 1867 Ontario, was one of the places P. M. Vankoughnet, commissioner of Crown lands, had instructed Haugan to highlight by distributing maps and pamphlets giving information about its promises as a place of settlement.

Christopher O. Closter, brother to Asbjørn Kloster, also became a member of the Society of Friends. Closter emigrated to Canada in 1848 with his wife, Bertha Elisabeth, and their sons, John, Richard, and Albert, and daughter, Anne. In the 1860 report, Buchanan states that he had sent Closter as an agent and Canadian civil servant to Norway to secure as many new "valuable settlers" as possible. During his ten or more years as a resident of Canada prior to returning to the homeland as an agent, Closter had engaged in a number of activities, among these starting a ship broker firm with Anton Jorgensen in Quebec; the firm offered to provide lumber freight to Norwegian shipowners. Jorgensen served as the foreign interpreter for the government immigration office; his agitation for Norwegian immigrants and his pamphlet on the emigration from Europe have been discussed earlier. In a report to Buchanan in 1864, Jorgensen described Norwegian immigrants as belonging to "a fine, hardy race" and encouraged actions by Canadian authorities to retain as many of them as possible. In addition to his collaborative business enterprise with Jorgensen, Closter served during the 1858 immigration season in Buchanan's official quarters as Norwegian interpreter at the port of Quebec. The letterhead of correspondence, in Norwegian, from Closter's office on Napoleon Wharf in Quebec—"Canada: Regjeringens Emigrations-Departement for Norske og Svenske" (The Government's Emigration Department for Norwegians and Swedes)—suggests the distinctive nature of his responsibility and the predominance of Norwegian emigrants, who are listed ahead of the Swedes. His undertakings as emigration and settlement broker, both successes and failures, will be considered later.[3]

ACROSS THE DEEP BLUE SEA

Canada sought not only settlers but traffic through Canada as well. On July 24, 1850, an act was passed "to encourage Emigrants from Europe to the United States to use the St. Lawrence Route." The benefits to those who chose this route included a rebate: "it shall be lawful for the Governor to instruct the collector of customs at any port or ports on or near the frontier between this province and the United States to pay back . . . a sum equal to one-half of the duty paid upon any emigrant arriving in the province after the 1st day of May; provided . . . that such emigrant came into this province with the declared intention of passing directly through it to the United States." The landing tax levied in New York was much higher than the rate paid in Quebec—one more reason to choose the latter destination. The 1850 report further states, "This law has been acted upon in one instance this year, the case of a party of Norwegians, (the first that have ever arrived at this port), per ship 'Lyna,' from Drammen, who all proceeded to Chicago."

Chief emigration agent Buchanan also reported the arrival of *Lyna* in 1850 as the first Norwegian vessel with passengers to land in Quebec. In his brief account of the emigration, historian Nils Vigeland devotes considerable space to describe the challenges and ordeals of the Atlantic crossing on sailing ships: "A journey on a large, modern emigrant steamship has nothing in common with a voyage across the Atlantic on the old sailing ships that took passengers over to Quebec or other cities on the eastern coast. The emigrants were packed together onboard these small vessels about like cattle, had to do without all conveniences and suffered so much hardship that one today may ask how they on the whole endured."

The sailing ships were not constructed to carry passengers; as a consequence people emigrating might disrespectfully be spoken of as "cargo" and even "hick cargo" (*dølalast*), in reference to those from distant dales thought of as being awkward. During the winter months when the ships were laid up—as Alfred Petersen Wright relates from the city of Porsgrunn about his father, shipowner P. M. Petersen, and his engagement in the emigrant-timber traffic—they were furnished for the emigrant traffic to Quebec. The entire interior space was equipped with a deck of planks on the between deck beams, with hatches down to the room below where all luggage was stored. Bunks were placed on both sides the entire length of the ship in two heights, one above the other; they were sufficiently wide to let three to four people lie next to each other. In front of the bunks there was a bench. On some vessels there was room for the emigrant's chest in front of the bunk. Special bunks might be placed midships for passengers with greater demands. Arrangements might vary according to the size of the ship, however. Most ships also had one or more cabins on deck for the more affluent passengers. Shipowner P. M. Petersen in 1859 announced about his vessel, *Amelia*, "As the ship has two cabins and several chambers in these, there is an excellent opportunity to take along cabin passengers." For passengers traveling between deck, or in steerage, there were no separate rooms for men and women. Light came through open hatches or glass in the deck; fresh air was provided through the

This image drawn in 1861 shows the crowded, unhealthy, and primitive conditions in steerage on sailing ships of that era. The Atlantic crossing might take from six to eight weeks. From *Det var engang* (1944). *Courtesy of Fredrik Bockelie, Nesbru, Norway*

open hatches. But in bad weather the hatches had to be covered, creating stifling conditions without light below deck; only a couple of lamps burned night and day down in the contaminated air and filth.

There were, however, also lighter moments. In good weather, the emigrants gathered on deck, and, if there was a fiddler or accordion player on board, people might engage in mirthful traditional folk dances like *halling, springar,* or *vossarull* or simply enjoy a concert; if there was no musical instrument, they made use of a song with tempo and musical tone. These much-appreciated activities made the voyage less tedious. Clara Jacobson relates from her voyage from Drammen on the ship *Tegner* in 1853 that people from town and surroundings waltzed and schottisched. The human spirit cannot easily be quelled, even in adversity. "A jovial boy from Valdres," Jacobson tells, "amused himself by mimicking the dance of the city folks. He wore a red stocking cap which swung back and forth as he turned around in his solo dance." As soon as the passengers disembarked, the entire furnishing between deck was removed, and the loading of timber for England began.

There was a single galley for the passengers where everyone prepared their own food. The emigrants had to provide their own rations and bedding. While cabin passengers frequently dined with the captain, firewood and water were supplied by the shipowner. Great quantities of provisions had to be transported from the emigrants' home communities to the port city where they would embark. A transportation contract determined the responsibilities of the ship's owner and captain and the passengers. Before leaving port, the provisions had to be judged adequate for ten to twelve weeks. Ole Rynning in 1838 gave the following advice in his book, *True Account of America:* "The provisions for the sea voyage should include a supply of every kind of food which can be kept a long time without being spoiled. One ought to take with him pork, dried meat, salted meat, dried herring, smoked herring, dried fish, butter, cheese, primost [cheese from skim milk], milk, beer, flour, peas, cereals, potatoes, rye rusks, coffee, tea, sugar, pots, pans, and kettles."

The ship captains and owners were obligated to abide by both Norwegian law and the ordinances that applied at Canadian ports. Norwegian ships frequently exceeded the Canadian ordinance regarding the number of passengers relative to the ship's tonnage, and the ships were confiscated. The Swedish-Norwegian consul then had to intervene and negotiate a lower fine and release of the ship. As an example, in 1862 the brig *Oscar den 1ste* from the small Norwegian town of Åsgårdstrand in Vestfold *fylke* was fined $65.80. "After many circumstances," the consul reported, "I succeeded in having the fine reduced to 42 dollars and 5 cents on account of the ship's tonnage after new measurements turned out to be somewhat larger than first stated at the customs house."

Norwegian authorities also wished to exercise control over the transportation of emigrants and to improve conditions on board. Their actions were directed against the practice of transporting both passengers and goods on the same vessel. The May 23, 1863, "Law Concerning Transportation of Passengers, Destined to Foreign Continents" (*Lov angaaende Fart med Passagerer, bestemte til fremmede Verdensdele*) required, "The place . . . that is designated for passengers, should provide them with a sufficient amount of air and light in addition to adequate protection against moisture." The law listed cargo and ballast, such as "bad smelling and for the health harmful goods," that the vessel could not transport, referring to herring and dried cod, which the law required transported in compact containers that would not "cause any unpleasant smell for the passengers." The law also determined that each passenger should have a minimum area in the assigned part of the ship; it most importantly had a firm requirement in regard to the amount of fresh water on board. The 1863 law also required medical examination of the passengers to determine that all were healthy before the ship left port, stipulated required rescue means of one large lifeboat and two sloops, and ordered a maritime law inspection to determine that the ship was seaworthy. The law, in force until 1903, steadily improved conditions during the final years of the sailing ship era.

The aforementioned law of 1867 required agents to obtain permission from the chief of police in the city where they were headquartered and led to emigration protocols being kept by the police. The "Emigrant Ships Law"

(*Emigrantskipsloven*), as it is generally called, of 1869 expanded on the ordinance of 1867 and ordered agents to give emigrants a written contract informing them about terms, manner of transportation, and destination. The emigrants thus received a ticket all the way to their destination.[4]

The crossing to Quebec on a sailing ship might last from six to eight weeks, but the duration varied greatly, "depending on weather and wind, on luck and sailor competence." The *Hebe*, as mentioned earlier, became the exception, with a record of only four weeks to make the voyage across the Atlantic. Helge Nordvik found considerable variations between years and vessels in the sailing time from Norway to Quebec; normally, he states, the crossing lasted at least sixty days. The Norwegian Central Bureau of Statistics kept records from 1866 of the number of days of travel, and the Swedish-Norwegian consul reported on it. Sailing ships as a rule made only one trip each season; two trips turned out to be the exception, more so for passenger ships than for those engaged only in the Quebec timber trade and sailed-in ballast from Norway, which was done only by the larger vessels. Ships that did not compete for passenger cargo chose instead to sail early from Norway in ballast; they hoped to arrive in Quebec sufficiently early to make two trips of timber to Britain. The last trip to Europe, for the few ships that made a second voyage, was frequently feared, as the ships were exposed to autumn storms in October and November. Many a timber runner vanished on the way home.

Table 1 shows the number of Norwegian passengers disembarking from sailing vessels to the consular district of Quebec, 1850–74. The table lists steerage and cabin passengers and births during the voyage.[5]

The number of emigrants fluctuated greatly from year to year throughout the twenty-five years covered in Table 1. Chapter two considered the shifting migratory forces throughout Norway. The great majority of Norwegian sailing ships did not carry passengers. In 1871, for example, the Swedish-Norwegian consulate reported as many as 116 Norwegian ships, second only to the British; in comparison, there were only eight German, three Swedish, and two Danish calls on Quebec by sailing ships from these nations. The consul concluded that "Norwegian shipping is as usual very sizable," while "The Swedish shipping is as usual insignificant." Swedish emigration was also modest. The consulate recorded only 395 Swedish emigrants in 1862 compared to the much larger Norwegian figure. The number of Swedish immigrants arriving indirectly on steamships, however, increased toward the end of the period; in 1871, a total of 3,500 Swedish emigrants compared to 2,875 Norwegian emigrants disembarked from steamers in Quebec.

The table includes only arrivals directly from a Norwegian port to Quebec. Norwegian vessels with emigrants also arrived at St. John in New Brunswick, Halifax in Nova Scotia, Gaspé in Gaspesia, and Montreal, but they were few compared to those arriving at Quebec. Consulates were opened in port cities where the landing of ships, either with passengers or in ballast, was sufficiently numerous to justify a diplomatic post; they were mainly honorary appointments. The Swedish-Norwegian consul resided in Quebec, a vice consul served in Montreal, and there were for shorter or longer periods as

TABLE 1: Number of Norwegian Passengers Disembarking from Sailing Vessels to the Consular District of Quebec, 1850–74 .

Year	Passengers	Year	Passengers
1850	244	1863	987
1851	225	1864	3,999
1852	2,197	1865	3,365
1853	5,056	1866	13,506
1854	5,586	1867	11,620
1855	1,267	1868	9,403
1856	2,806	1869	8,553
1857	6,123	1870	8,985
1858	2,389	1871	5,386
1859	1,715	1872	3,788
1860	1,781	1873	2,010
1861	8,406	1874	506
1862	4,949		

Total number of arriving Norwegian passengers 1850–74: 114,852 required vice consuls in ports such as Gaspé, St. John, Halifax, Three Rivers, and several other locations. Lars Erik Larson offers a detailed overview of Scandinavian emigrants landing in Quebec City and countries of departure. In 1859, Larson reports, 41 Norwegians arrived from Sweden and, in 1861, 261; 67 came from Britain in 1853 and 199 in 1854. These should be added to the total, which then becomes 115,420. The reports from "His Swedish and Norwegian Majesty's Consulate" in Quebec, as consulted by the author and cited by Jacob S. Worm-Müller, provide the following arrivals, in Table 2, of Norwegian emigrants by sail and steam. The consular figures vary somewhat from the official statistics listed in the previous table.

The majority of Norwegian emigrants who did not travel directly from Norway left from Liverpool to New York in the 1850s, but their numbers were small. Liverpool became the great port of departure for emigrants. There were early examples of Atlantic crossings by steamships, but it was not until the late 1840s that the movement gained impetus. Auxiliary steam power had been applied to sailing vessels many years before its use across the Atlantic. In Britain as well as Norway, as has been suggested, steam-powered ships were mainly limited to the coastal service, and, as construction and power

TABLE 2

Year	By sail from Norway to Quebec and Montreal	By steamship via Hull and Liverpool
1866	13,506	1,477
1867	11,620	(not available)
1868	9,590	1,112
1869	8,598	2,758
1870	8,990	7,772
1871	5,383	2,875
1872	3,812	1,128
1873	2,004	1,075
1874	506	894
Total 1866–74	64,009	19,091

improved, steamships also traveled to neighboring countries. Norwegian steamships had after 1827 regular runs on Gothenburg, Copenhagen, and Kiel, and from 1841 along the entire coast of Norway; private Norwegian steamship companies were established in the 1850s in order to secure regular traffic at the Hanseatic city Hamburg, Norway's most important foreign market at that time.

It is of interest to note that sailing vessels reached the peak in development at the very time they were being replaced in the passenger trade by steamships, the improvements spurred by the growing competition. Steamships had the great advantage to depart throughout the entire year; the hygienic conditions were also in general much better on board. Steerage in the early steamships was, however, not much different from that on sailing ships; bunks, for instance, were described as two-story shelves and generally not deep enough for a person to stretch out completely; improvements in steerage conditions came with new constructions, though crossing the Atlantic as a steerage passenger between decks could be unpleasant also on board the steamships. Norwegians began arriving by steamship in Quebec in 1862, mainly from Liverpool but also occasionally from a port city such as Glasgow or Southampton. The crossing from Liverpool to Quebec could be made in about two weeks, and departures were regular and announced in advance; provisions were covered as a part of the fare.[6]

Most of the Atlantic steamship lines left from Liverpool. The British Wilson Line gained a near monopoly on transporting emigrants from a Norwegian port to Hull. It had a regular route between Scandinavia and Hull as early as 1850; it expanded as traffic dictated, and by 1867 offered service from Oslo and a call at Kristiansand; it expanded routes to include Trondheim, with calls at Kristiansund and Ålesund and Bergen, with a stopover at Stavanger. The feeder services from Norway and Sweden to ports in England and Scotland established by the Allan Line and the Anchor Line were not profitable and soon abandoned. From Hull the emigrants took the train to Liverpool. They there were housed in lodgings operated by the individual steamship lines. From the late 1860s especially, the Allan Line, mentioned earlier, and the Inman, Guion, White Star, Anchor, and National Cunard lines competed for emigrants. They all had agencies in Oslo; the steamship lines had agents who would transport emigrants to the interior of the American continent. In addition, they all filled Norwegian newspapers with their advertising.

It might be of interest to note briefly that business interests in Oslo were still willing to invest in the traffic to Quebec by establishing a direct steamship connection. The well-known emigrant shipping company Ludvigsen and Schelderup together with business partners in 1872 purchased the steamship *Woodham* at an auction in England. They sought passengers by stressing the fact that the ship was Norwegian, that it had a Norwegian crew and a Norwegian doctor, and that "Food is according to Norwegian custom"; a reliable man would accompany the emigrants into the country and care for their needs and serve as interpreter. It departed from Oslo for Montreal in July 1872 and returned from there to Ireland with a load of grain. The Swedish-Norwegian consul in Quebec thought that the initiative boded well, but it in fact was *Woodham*'s single voyage with emigrants.

The destination for Norwegian emigrants again gradually became New York rather than Quebec. According to Norwegian reports in 1870, as an example, 14,838 Norwegian emigrants landed in New York; in the same year 8,990 landed in Quebec on a Norwegian sailing ship and 7,772 on a steamer from Liverpool. The first wave in Norwegian mass migration that began in 1866 ended abruptly in 1874. That year only 4,601 Norwegians landed in the United States, down from 10,352 the previous year; only 506 Norwegians arrived in Quebec by sail and 894 by steam. Beginning in 1875 Quebec and the other ports on the St. Lawrence waterway ceased having any significance in the emigrant trade; steamship passenger transportation had won the day, and the main destination from Europe was again New York.

Steamship passenger traffic between British ports and Canada continued. The royal mail steamer the Allan Line advertised its services in the Norwegian press and offered weekly crossings to Canada and the United States. As late as 1902, the line again reminded prospective passengers that "the seaway to

Halifax and Quebec is considerably shorter than to New York and Boston";
its newly acquired twin screw steamers, the *Bavarian* and the *Tunisian*, were
featured. Norwegian emigrants continued to land in Canadian ports, but
their numbers are difficult to determine due to missing and incomplete out-
bound passenger lists.

The American Emigrant Aid and Homestead Company's effort in 1866,
the same year as its founding in New York, to establish a direct steamship
line between Oslo and America resulted in only one crossing before the
company went bankrupt. Another short-lived initiative was made in 1871 by
Peter Jebsen and commercial interests in Bergen with the founding of the
Norwegian-American Steamship Company (*Det Norsk-Amerikanske Dampskibs-
selskab*). It had regular sailings to New York during the summer months until
1876. The Danish Thingvalla Line, begun in 1879, was a more successful
venture to capitalize on the lucrative Atlantic passenger transportation. It
established direct links from Scandinavia to the United States until 1898,
when it also lost out in this traffic to the financially superior British and
north German companies.[7]

Across the Ocean on the Bark *Valkyrien*

Exposed to fog, storms, and in early spring even floating masses of ice as the
vessels approached Newfoundland and the St. Lawrence waterway—causing
some for a time to be icebound—passenger ships did occasionally disappear
en route, but these instances were very few. Almost all made it across without damage, though there might be dramatic events along the way. Captain
Edvard Funnemark on the bark *Catarina* from Porsgrunn related how he and
his crew "the night between September 13 and 14 1858" at great risk to themselves and the ship rescued the passengers and crew of the German emigrant
steamship *Austria* on its way from Hamburg to Quebec; the ship was on
fire and sinking. "When the rescue was complete," he further recounted,
"there were many stirring scenes, showing the gratitude of the shipwrecked
people, as they clung to the ship's crew, embraced and thanked them for
the rescue." Shipwreck was much more common for ships in ballast west and

timber back than for ships carrying passengers, due to early crossings and attempts at two trips. In 1875 the Swedish-Norwegian consul in Quebec reported that thirty-nine Norwegian ships had suffered mishap at sea: seven foundered, two because of collision with ice on their voyage west and being abandoned by the crew, and five by being stranded. No human life was lost, however.

The bark *Valkyrien* was only five years old when, on April 25, 1873, it sailed out from Bergen for Quebec City. The bark's captain was A. Müller, earlier captain of *Fædre Minde*, and the vessel carried 303 Norwegian emigrants. Some writers have mistakenly contended that *Valkyrien* was the last Norwegian sailing ship to transport passengers across the Atlantic; there were in fact two crossings with emigrants the following year: in 1874 the bark *Brødrene* sailed from Stavanger and the ship *Pontecorvo* from Oslo. Together they transported 506 emigrants to Quebec. Between the sailing of the sloop *Restauration* from Stavanger in 1825 and the two vessels in 1874 lay forty-nine years—nearly half a century—of Norwegian passenger traffic across the Atlantic by sailing ships.

The dramatic crossing by *Valkyrien* in 1873 makes for an apt concluding commentary on the end of an era. The vessel landed in Quebec sixty-three days after it left Bergen. The voyage began with a bad omen: an escaped prisoner hid on board, delaying the departure for four hours until one of the emigrants offered to pay the mortgage debt that had placed the man in prison; he was then allowed to emigrate with the other passengers. But there was also a thief on board; the disappearance of people's provisions led to appointment of a quartermaster, who assumed ownership of the key to the storage room. The emigrants were permitted to get supplies once every twenty-four hours.

Misfortunes persisted. Three days after leaving Bergen, *Valkyrien* collided with a brigantine in the middle of the night; the lanterns in the rigging were not as visible as in ordinary weather, and the other ship could not see them. There was high sea, and *Valkyrien*, greatly damaged, was flooded. The captain ordered everyone on deck in order to get into the lifeboats. The passengers panicked, some being unable to make it up to the deck. With the help of the pumps and a canvas, the crew kept the waves from washing over the ship; they set what sails they could and headed down the English Channel. Seeing land, the crew boosted the pilot flag, and a pilot boat approached; the high sea hindered it from coming alongside, and the pilot had to jump and be pulled on board *Valkyrien* with a line.

With the current and the wind, *Valkyrien* drifted toward the French coast; its distress flag was observed in the channel city of Dover. A steamship sent out to the disabled vessel pulled it to shore. A local shipyard repaired the damages; *Valkyrien* was laid up for ten days. During this time, the emigrants were well received and made many new friends. People from town came on board with gifts of food. One of the visitors was a pastor of Norwegian descent who arranged for a party for the passengers and the crew.

Valkyrien departed Dover on May 9; there was no wind, and the vessel was pulled out of port by a steamship. The current thereafter carried it slowly to Folkestone, just south of Dover, where it anchored after thirty hours. While there a twenty-month-old boy from Bergen died.

The ship passed Ireland on May 15 and sailed into the stormy Atlantic Ocean. Seasickness prevailed. Many women went to bed and refused to come up on deck. Captain Müller ordered every man to bring his wife up for fresh air, weather permitting, and offered to help if the man could not do it alone. As enticement, he persuaded some musicians to give an improvised concert. As the story goes, the blissful tones brought many out of bed and up on deck. The storm continued, shutting off the lanterns on the port side, which nearly caused a collision with a passing schooner, a hazard prevented only when a big wave sent the ships away from each other.

On June 4, *Valkyrien* came to the Newfoundland banks; it passed three icebergs to the west. The weather improved, and on June 15 the bark approached the mouth of the St. Lawrence River and the pilot flag was hoisted; in order to alert the pilot to their presence, the crew signaled with primitive rockets. After the pilot was on board, *Valkyrien* sailed to the quarantine station on Grosse Île; there the examining doctor came on board. All were well, and the visiting physician could soon leave the ship. It continued on to Quebec, and on June 20 the emigrants bade farewell to *Valkyrien* and the crew, who in their honor had raised nineteen flags and together with the officers saluted them.[8]

Grosse Île

Grosse Île is described in the literature as the "Gateway to Canada 1832–1937." It is a small island in the St. Lawrence River about thirty miles downstream from Quebec City. In 1832 it became the location of a quarantine station for cholera victims in order to prevent entry of a British epidemic to North America; it in addition provided a place for the inspection of ships coming up the river. The name *grosse*, meaning "big," may seem misleading. It was named not because of its size but because of its height, which made it visible to arriving ships. All ships approaching Grosse Île were obligated to stop for inspection at the place marked by buoys. If anyone on board had been in contagion, the river pilots had to bring the ships to anchor with, according to the regulations, "a blue flag flying at the fore top-gallant masthead." Small boats went out with medical inspectors and returned with the sick passengers and their baggage; a deep sea wharf was built only in 1866. There was a large receiving hall, hospitals, and several doctors. The quarantined were released when considered well. Medical knowledge at that time was at an elemental stage, however, and the medical facilities were limited and did not meet demands. The emigrants themselves arrived in poor physical condition, lacking resistance to the virulent diseases they were exposed to. It was a reoccurring situation. If the vessels needed cleansing, all passengers had to come ashore. The cholera epidemic of 1832 did strike, causing many deaths.

The Irish famine migration of 1847 created an even more fearful period on Grosse Île. The potato crop failure in Ireland led to a well-documented famine. Both government and private measures to feed the population were inadequate, and people chose emigration as one solution. Since the tenants were no longer profitable, landlords encouraged them to leave, even assisting financially. Immigrant ships from Ireland and Liverpool "carried throngs of the malnourished, downtrodden, dispirited people, ravaged by hunger and

A view of the quarantine station at Grosse Île. *National Archives of Canada. Courtesy of Lars Erik Larson*

disease . . . particularly typhus." Grosse Île, where the ships landed, did not have adequate hospital capacity. There were many deaths on the ships and after the emigrants came ashore, and burials became unceremonious. The chapel of St. Luke on the island included reports like "I, the undersigned priest, have this day buried Patrick Murphy, John Kelly, Maria Brown and forty-three others." During the summer of sorrow, between May 10 and July 24, 1847, as statistics recorded, 1,458 died in the hospital; of these 467 were children, 416 women, and 575 men. Another 2,366 died on ships from Great Britain, 751 on ships at Grosse Île, and 27 in tents near the facilities of the healthy arrivals. A total of 4,572 perished during these few weeks. The deaths left a large number of orphans. On August 15, 1909, an Irish monument was consecrated to commemorate the victims of the famine migration. Set on a prominent site and surmounted by a Celtic cross, the monument attains a height of forty-eight feet.

Emigrants from many nations landed at Grosse Île; immigration was heavy until World War I. From the 1850s, of course, Norway was a large contributor to the body of arriving immigrants. Canadian authorities employed a German and a Norwegian interpreter to stay on the island during the yearly emigration season from April 1 until the end of November. Andrew Andersen, an emigrant from Stavanger, joined the police force on the quarantine island in the mid-1850s; he was later promoted to interpreter. In a letter dated April 20, 1868, he petitions the Honorable Minister of Emigration and Agriculture at Ottawa for a position as interpreter at the government emigration office in Quebec. His statement says much about a Norwegian presence:

> Sir, the Petitioner having been in the Service of the Government for the last 15 years, 12 years stationed at Quarantine in Grosse Ile and 3 years in the Government Emigration Office in Quebec, and, having been informed in

From the officer's quarters on Grosse Île. *National Archives of Canada. Courtesy of Lars Erik Larson*

consequence of the unusually large immigration of Norwegian passengers to Canada this year, that a Norwegian interpreter is required at the Emigration Office in Quebec . . . I humbly ask Your Honor to consider my long servitude to the Government at a very small salary. That you will grant me the favor of an appointment as Norwegian Interpreter, even at a small salary.

Christopher Closter had served as interpreter at the emigration office from 1858; he was succeeded by his former business associate A. Jorgensen, who continued in that position until his death on October 6, 1866. Andrew Andersen was in 1868 competing with another applicant whom he identified only as "belonging to a forwarding agency" and serving temporarily as interpreter; he was likely the aforementioned John Holfeldt. Andersen had unsuccessfully sought the position in 1866 while serving as interpreter on Grosse Île; he then had the endorsement of the medical superintendent Frederick Montizambert, who described how Andersen had assisted him in the inspection of Norwegian vessels and how he had found Andersen to be "most efficient in every way." Andersen apparently got the position in 1868. He married a woman of Irish descent, Julia Cannon from Quebec. In 1881 he was still listed in the regional census as an interpreter.

Andersen is, as statistics show, correct in stressing the great increase in arrivals from Norway following the Civil War. Jorgensen, in his book of 1865, makes observations about mortality on the voyage of Norwegian sailing ships coming to Grosse Île, finding it to be greater than on any other vessels. "While on average," he observes, "only 5 died among every 1000 of other Emigrants, the Norwegian mortality amounted to 21." In his report for 1857, A. C. Buchanan concludes, "The greatest mortality occurred among the Norwegians, being 100 on an emigration of 6,507, or equal to 1.53 percent." It was in particular small children who died.

Jorgensen attributes the situation partly to overfilled ships, as well of course to the unsanitary conditions on board. Contagious illnesses, such as dysentery, or other epidemic diseases like cholera, typhus, and the typhus-like "ship fever," might spread quickly. Captain H. Cock-Jensen relates from the voyage of the bark *Laurvig* in the cholera year 1854 how the disease spread: "It began in the top bunk stern and continued forward sequentially on the starboard side until it jumped over on the port side and there was transmitted precisely the same way . . . Then death began to ravage." In all, thirteen people died; each deceased was laid in a nailed-together coffin and lowered into the sea in a simple but gripping ceremony. Those who died after the ship had entered the St. Lawrence waterway were buried on Grosse Île.

Jorgensen considers especially the high mortality rate during the years 1861 and 1862. In 1861 as many as 8,406 emigrants left Norway for Quebec on forty sailing ships; on the way 175 people died and 11 were quarantined. Of these, 103 died on eight ships that all carried passengers above the allowed number. The worst single instance occurred in 1862, when a ship from Porsgrunn with 280 passengers had 49 deaths during the voyage; 120 were taken to the emigrant hospital in Quebec, where 31 died, a total loss of 80 passengers. The immigration report in the British Parliamentary Papers for the year 1862 has the following conclusion: "Of the Norwegians there died

The last journey: a burial on board. Picture taken ca. 1917 at Buenos Aires, Argentina. *Photo by Ingard Henriksen. Norsk maritimt museum, Oslo Norway*

184 on the passage and 42 in quarantine, making together 226, or more than four percent of the whole number. Among the Germans, there died 77 at sea and 15 in hospital. The diseases which proved so fatal were small-pox, scarlet fever, and ship fever, fostered by the crowded state of some vessels, and by the absence, as it is alleged, of the most simple precautions for health."

The Norwegian law of May 23, 1863, concerning transportation of passengers to foreign continents, represented a legislative response to these losses. Thereafter the mortality rate sank due to improvements on the sailing ships but even more so because steamships with their better sanitary conditions were taking over the overseas traffic, displacing the sailing ships. After the change to steamship transportation via Liverpool, Norwegians transported directly from Norway on sailing ships usually accounted for the majority of those detained in quarantine. For 1871 the Quebec consulate reported that health conditions on board had been good; only thirteen people had died in passage and of these nine on the same ship.

Both a Catholic chapel, St. Luke, and an Anglican chapel existed on Grosse Île; a Catholic priest and an Anglican minister were residents during the navigation season. They were devoted to the emigrants and officiated at marriages and baptisms; one of their services related to the many deaths, and thousands of funerals were conducted between 1832 and 1937, although few after World War I. Memorials have been raised on the island's cemeteries. They are touching sites. One erected in 1997 provides the names of 8,339 people of various nationalities who were buried on Grosse Île, the majority from Ireland. Among the names are also many Norwegians. They all awaken a deep and moving sense of the human sacrifice exacted of people who long ago sought a better life somewhere else.[9]

Entering Canada

Baron (*friherre*) Alfred Falkenberg, with a military background in Sweden, served as Swedish and Norwegian consul in Quebec from 1855. He was succeeded in about 1870 by Wilhelm Anthony Schwartz. Baron Falkenberg was the main diplomatic contact for Swedish and Norwegian emigrants entering

Canada. In his annual reports to the Norwegian government, he provides an account of both trade and the composition of the Norwegian emigrant population for that year. Falkenberg in his 1869 report compares the emigrant population to Norway's own in regard to gender and age and concludes that the main difference is that among the emigrants the percentage of men in their years of work is relatively much greater than the homeland's.

A table prepared by Lars Larson in his study of the emigration covers Norwegian arrivals in Quebec for the period 1853 to 1874 and shows—with the exception of the years 1854 and 1867—that while the percentage of adult male emigrants, among all passengers fifteen years or older, landing in Quebec in 1853 was 56.2, adult female emigrants that year accounted for 43.8 percent of all passengers in the same category. The percentage for women emigrants remained in the mid-forties, moving closer to 50 percent in 1870–74. Even though men dominated percentagewise, the gender balance is much greater than one might have expected. The percentage of children fourteen years or younger amounted to 32 percent of the total number of emigrants in 1853; for some years it rose to about 36 percent. These statistics give the impression of a persistent family migration, although, as noted, there were also many young single emigrants. Both for men and women the largest emigrating age group was between the ages of twenty and twenty-four; thereafter followed the age groups twenty-five to twenty-nine and fifteen to nineteen. The 1866 consular report from Quebec indicates an age distinction between passengers on sailing ships and on steamships. "Many unfettered persons," young single people, in other words, chose the indirect route, while the emigration of families in general took place on sailing ships.

Statistical occupational information on male emigrants was not collected in Norway until 1868 and for female emigrants only beginning in 1903. It was, however, a heavily rural migration; even for the years 1866–70, 86 percent of all emigrants from Norway to North America—Canada and the United States—left from the countryside. They were for the most part common rural people, belonging to the class of low economic and social rank; there were, however, especially in the 1860s, prosperous farmers from eastern

Norway among the emigrants. More often the emigrants were small farmers, tenant farmers, cotters, craftsmen, or day laborers and in general in poor financial circumstances. The manifest of passengers on individual ships might list the following: name, age, sex, occupation, and destination. Frequently only name, age, and sex are given. The bark *Anna Delius* left Oslo for Quebec on April 29, 1867, with 410 passengers. By far the largest number of men were listed as laborers, a category that clearly included a variety of livelihoods; there were also farmers on board, artisans, butchers, a carpenter, a blacksmith, a painter, a shoemaker, a hatmaker, a spoonmaker, a tailor, and a beer brewer. Women's occupations are not given, but four women are identified as widows; there were two births during the voyage and four children died. A laborer, one Peder Hansen, was at seventy-three years the oldest person on the ship; there were seven in their sixties and several more in their fifties. The great majority were in their twenties and thirties, not counting the nearly 150 children fourteen years or younger. Financing the tickets for wife and children was a heavy lift for most emigrants; prepaid tickets from emigrated kin became the solution for an increasing number of them.

Many emigrants, nevertheless, landed penniless in Quebec and needed help and care. Canadian authorities might be called on to come to the rescue of passengers even before the ship docked. On July 11, 1868, assistant emigration agent L. Stafford telegraphed from the government emigration office in Quebec to port authorities the following: "Norwegian ship *Victoria* with three hundred & fifteen (315) passengers reported off Anticosti [Island] second July short of provisions. Fifteen (15) deaths. I have seen Consul [Falkenberg]. He will send provisions if Government sends steamer. The *Lady Head* is here & could leave in a few hours if ordered." *Victoria* left Oslo April 29 and made it safely to port on July 16 after having received assistance. An unusually long transit across the Atlantic explains why the ship ran out of provisions. It was not the only such incident the government dealt with during the shipping season.

After the many weeks together on a strenuous voyage, there was often a farewell event, as seen in the landing of *Valkyrien*, before the passengers stepped ashore in Quebec. Most captains took time to help the emigrants after landing. In addition to the Swedish-Norwegian consul, the emigrant agent Buchanan might very well be the first person who welcomed the emigrants. Protecting emigrants when they arrived was one of the main purposes of his office. Exposed to "runners" for boardinghouses and forwarding firms, the emigrants might easily become victims of swindle and extortion.[10]

Many arrived without means to pay for lodging or fares inland or to the American Midwest. In his 1866 report, Buchanan blames the situation on "false representation of shipping agents and other persons in Norway, interested in passenger traffic." He continues, "A considerable number of these poor people were induced to take passage to Quebec without having the means of proceeding farther on their journey under the assurance that they would be sent to their destination, by this Department, free of charge." The Canadian government incurred heavy expense as it assisted the indigent poor "of almost every Norwegian ship to reach the American Frontier." In 1866 Buchanan made the subject a special report, which through the Swedish and Norwegian consulate would encourage Norway to stop the shipping agents' fraud in the future. He had himself with some success detained the baggage of emigrants as security for their passage money. The aforementioned Emigrant Ships Law of 1869, ordering the agents to provide the emigrants a ticket all the way to their destination, i.e., a "through ticket," represented a legislative endeavor to address the problem.

Buchanan had as early as 1854 in letters translated into Norwegian and printed in Norwegian American newspapers as well as in Norway announced that poor emigrants from Norway, and "partly from other countries," without means to pay the expenses to make it to their destination had become a great burden. "Consequently," he announced, "will no one on account of poverty receive free transportation from here." The government fund in support of the emigration office would from then on exclusively be used "for the provisions and healing of the sick." That in itself was an openhearted use of resources. However, government funds granted to the emigration office continued to assist indigent emigrants to reach their destination. In 1859 147 Norwegians are reported as recipients. According to the 1866 report, the percentage of Norwegians receiving free passage substantially exceeded their percentage of the total number of immigrants landing in Quebec. However, there was soon by legislative fiat a stricter enforcement, as indicated in Buchanan's report for the year 1868, issued by the Dominion of Canada, which had been established the previous year. The policy of providing assistance to destitute foreign, mainly Norwegian and German, emigrants was discontinued.

Reduction of the parliamentary grant for immigration purposes ended the practice of allowing free transport to foreign pauper emigrants, as they are described, who landed at Quebec on their way to "the Western States of the Union." The 1868 report describes how impoverished emigrants lacking means to continue were housed in sheds on the wharf and suffered great discomfort; they were supplied daily by the emigration office with necessary provisions. Those with "through tickets" continued on immediately, and others with means negotiated transportation with the competing forwarding companies. Some of the indigent families received financial help from their friends and relatives in the United States and left for their destinations; others were assisted by private charity, such as the Quebec Emigrant Society. Fellow passengers might also chip in to help pay the travel expenses of their less-fortunate compatriots. Some of the captains of arriving vessels had, even prior to the legislative order, paid for the transport of their poor, and as the report states, "did so in all cases" so that their passengers should not suffer inconvenience or detention. Other captains simply landed them and left them to fend for themselves.

The solicitor general for the province of Quebec in 1868 sent at the expense of the shipowner "ninety souls, (a portion of the destitute poor), from the Norwegian ship 4de November, which arrived 16th August . . . to the Eastern Townships." The report concluded on a positive note by claiming that most of the "souls" had settled in the townships and "appear to be satisfied with their prospects." The Prussian and the Norwegian consuls replied when informed of the needs of destitute emigrants of their nationalities that they had no authority to render any assistance. But the situation apparently improved.

In his 1871 report, Wilhelm Anthony Schwartz, the new Swedish-Norwegian consul in Quebec, noted that "Any destitution or shortages have not been detected among the emigrants, and they have all been in possession of the necessary funds to cover their travel expenses through the country."

Emigrant aid societies existed in Quebec and Montreal; there was also, as in Quebec, an emigration office in the latter city. The Quebec Emigrant Society was founded as early as 1818 to "look after the throngs of immigrants who landed, in increasing numbers, every summer on the docks of Quebec"—at that time, mainly from Great Britain and Ireland. The society provided advice and information as well as shelter and food. Its principal role, however, apparently was to assist the immigrants with passage to the interior, upriver to Montreal and beyond, to where they were destined for settlement. The Montreal Emigrant Society was founded in 1831 and offered relief, helped to secure employment, and arranged transportation to areas of settlement. This assistance given to impoverished emigrants continued alongside that of other benevolent societies.[11]

In selection of the most desirable immigrants for the Dominion of Canada, Mauri A. Jalava, archivist for the Finnish Canadian Cultural Federation, maintains that Canadian authorities were strongly influenced by the prevalent doctrines of social Darwinism and Anglo-Saxonism. A selective immigration policy created an idealized image of the Scandinavian, or Nordic, emigrants as having the perfect virtues of the ideal settler. In this view, Nordic people were second only to Anglo-Saxons, a thought-provoking assessment. Certainly Canadian immigration agents, government officials, and businessmen eagerly sought emigrants from the Scandinavian countries, most specifically from Norway and Iceland, in competition with other host countries such as the United States. Railroad companies and steamship lines advocated immigration, and industrial interests of many kinds made demands on the labor force that immigrants provided.

Immigration in general was viewed by Canadians as being highly desirable in spurring economic growth and in developing the country's infrastructure. The promotion of immigration began in 1854 when the Province of Canada, formed in 1841, appropriated funds to that end. In its immigration work, as already has been suggested, Canada depended heavily on the publication and distribution of pamphlets.

The great majority of Nordic immigrants came from the Kingdom of Norway. The pamphlet published in 1856 was translated into Norwegian, German, and French; five thousand copies were sent to Norway. The pamphlet published in 1857, titled "Canada: A Brief Outline of Her Geographical Position, Productions, Climate, Capabilities, Educational and Municipal Institutions," was for a decade or more revised almost annually. It was printed in countless numbers in the languages listed above, as well as in English, and was distributed lavishly in Great Britain, Ireland, and Norway. A second initiative, sending agents to Great Britain, Norway, and other European countries, became a major campaign.

Canada was not, however, profiting greatly from promoting immigration and settlement. Most of the immigrants arriving in Quebec and Montreal went directly to the United States. In 1856 A. C. Buchanan estimated that "the whole of our Norwegian emigration—one-half the Germans and Irish—and about one-sixth of those from England and Scotland, have proceeded to the United States." It was a number that equaled nearly 42 percent of all arrivals, "leaving," Buchanan concluded, "the number of actual settlers in the Province, at 24,816 souls." Development of the "through ticket system" by the ship and rail forwarding and ticket agents allowed emigrants to purchase their entire ship and rail passage before leaving their homelands and compounded Canada's disadvantaged position in retaining emigrants. The total number of emigrants arriving in Canada was for many years in excess of the capacity of the country to absorb, however. The government consequently adopted measures to encourage those who in its opinion were the more desirable people to emigrate and settle there.[12]

ABANDONING SHIP

The Quebec consular report for 1871 reported 167 "deserters" in the district, 103 of them when their ship docked in the port of Quebec. Norwegian seamen's desertion from the merchant fleet began to be a serious problem for Norwegian shipping by the mid-1800s. Historian Johan Nicolay Tønnesen in his analysis of the situation maintains that "It is without question historically most valid to view the desertion as a factor in Norwegian emigration." This underhanded and illegal emigration eluded accurate official statistics, and the accessible statistical records of the number of deserters are consequently very incomplete; the consular estimates tend to be higher than the rosters of the chief enlister.

The number of merchant sailors jumping ship increased during the 1860s and 1870s, reflecting the great expansion in Norwegian shipping. In the period 1861–65, officials complained that "there is a steady stream of workers from the rural communities to the coastal towns where they easily get berth on a ship and desert." Similar concerns had been expressed earlier. The reasons for deserting might vary and might have both an individual and a social component; some saw their employ on board simply as free transportation to America. The most significant cause of desertion was, however, the great difference between Norwegian and foreign wages, especially the English and American. Many seamen left ship in England, but even more did so in New York, and the situation was not much better in Canada. Members of the crew abandoned ship in many ports, as reported by the vice consuls, but most in the port of Quebec. Consul Schwartz showed great interest in the desertion problem and gave detailed information about the issue in his annual reports. His 1871 account stated that he considered it impossible to prevent desertion as long as Quebec did not become a port of discharge, i.e., one where seamen signed off and on ships. In 1870, as an example, 107 Norwegian sailors had deserted in Quebec City; from the entire district 164 had left, greater numbers than the previous year, when 164 sailors had deserted from 266 ship calls. Desertion was a constant problem faced by shipowners and captains.

Loading and unloading cargo was a lengthy process in the era of sailing ships, and after landing the crews stayed in town for one or more weeks. As a result, dockside sailortowns came into being. Prostitution, drinking establishments, and entertainments flourished in towns such as Quebec and Montreal and had a presence elsewhere; it was all offered to seafarers with money and time to kill. Prostitution created problems. In the large port cities, the women were lined up on the dock, often in front of a circle of barrooms and dives. It became a minefield for the seaman to traverse; his stay on land might otherwise be reduced to a drink and a visit to a brothel, the latter with the risk of life-threatening infections. Historian Judith Fingard has studied the sailortowns in the seaports of Quebec, St. John, and Halifax during the shipping season in the age of sail; there, "sailors sought work, jumped ship, created disturbances, and fought for a better work environment." They were induced to leave their vessels by the crimps for which Quebec was especially notorious. Crimping, or entrapping sailors, was made illegal in Canada in 1847. The crimps operated specialized sailors' boardinghouses which became the headquarters of their illegal operations; runners, the crimp's hired hands, often seamen who had themselves deserted, did the dirty work. It might involve shanghaiing the sailor and by various means preventing him from boarding his ship before it left port and thereafter forcing him aboard another vessel. And there were Norwegians among the crimps. The *Morning Herald* in Halifax reported on July 31, 1884, that "yesterday Hendrick Gullicksen, proprietor of a sailors' boarding home on Water Street and [his runner] Peter Hendricksen, both Norwegian, were arrested under warrants charging them with stealing sailors." Both men were convicted and sentenced to three months in jail. The crimps, stigmatized as sailor stealers, were agents or brokers who boldly promised sailors superior wages on vessels or on land and promised hard-pressed sea captains much-needed crew members. The expanding British and American as well as Norwegian fleets created a great demand for merchant seamen.

The men jumping ship were young, many on their first voyage; of the 346 who in 1860–64 abandoned ship from the Bergen hiring district in Great Britain, the United States, Canada, and the Netherlands, 13 were in the age group fourteen to seventeen, 197 eighteen to twenty-three, and 96 twenty-four to twenty-nine. Perhaps the youth of many deserters made them easier victims for the crimps. Every year a substantial number of the deserted sailors

RUNNERS OF THE OLDEN TIME.

Immigrants and sailors jumping ship were exposed to swindle and trickery by
runners and crimps who worked for boardinghouses, forwarding companies,
railroads, and other establishments. *Harper's Weekly*, June 26, 1858

returned to Norway. The majority of those who jumped ship were not taken
by the boarding masters to other ships but found employment inland on
railroad construction and as sailors on the Great Lakes, where they replaced
retiring sailors. Others were hired as seamen on American coastal vessels.
And Norwegian seamen were important in manning the Canadian merchant
marine. In the period 1863–1913, almost six percent of all men who ever crewed
a Canadian deep-sea vessel were born in Norway; more than 27,000 Norwegians likely sailed in the Atlantic Canadian fleet during this half century.[13]

The Bury Settlement

Bury township is located in the Eastern Townships some twenty-four miles
east of the city of Sherbrooke. The region of Quebec Province south of the

St. Lawrence River that was unconceded at the time of the Great Conquest is defined as the Eastern Townships; it is a landscape of hills and fertile valleys, traversed by mountain ranges and intersected by rivers that flow from picturesque lakes. The land was owned by the British American Land Company with headquarters in Sherbrooke. Early settlers could reach Sherbrooke by way of the city of Three Rivers (Trois-Rivières), located at the confluence of the St. Lawrence and the Saint-Maurice rivers. A railroad connection to the Eastern Townships existed from the early 1850s; Bury was the name of the railroad station and the municipality.

Bury became the site of the first Norwegian settlement in the province. Norwegian-born Cornelius H. Tambs was appointed as agent by the British American Land Company to serve among his countrymen. The company had nearly 500,000 acres to sell, "in quantities to suit all classes of settlers, from 50 acres upwards." The history of Norwegian settlements in Quebec Province relies on the official emigrant reports as main sources. The 1854 account relates that two Norwegians had settled in the Bury region the previous year. Their favorable reports to their compatriots soon attracted a party of fourteen Norwegian families, comprising fifty to sixty people, who arrived in Quebec from Oslo on the ship *Flora* on June 4, 1854; the newcomers acquired some property in the township. Chief agent Buchanan entertained great hopes, as he wrote, that this, the first party of Norwegians of any consequence to have established themselves in Canada, would prove "a valuable acquisition to that important section of the province." He was convinced that the Norwegian settlers would be successful and that others would follow.

Cornelius Tambs had property in Bury; he also promoted settlement and assisted Norwegian settlers in finding employment. Emigrant agent Helge Haugan had for some time been a resident of Bury, and though he failed as a farmer, he did, as Buchanan stressed in 1860, become "acquainted with the soil, climate, and resources of the Province." Johan Schrøder in his travels in the United States and Canada in 1863 visited Bury and related that Haugan in 1862 had sold his three hundred acres of forest land, having cleared forty acres, and moved to Montreal with his large family. He was, Schrøder notes, "convinced that he had made the right selection of land for his countrymen."

Martin Ulvestad, in his brief account of Bury, erroneously makes John Svendsen, a sea captain from Risør, Norway, in 1857 the first settler and thus the Norwegian colony's founder in the same year the British American Land Company commenced settlement. Tambs had in 1857 convinced ninety settlers who landed in Quebec to accompany him to Bury; in June some young Norwegian men were sent to the area because they had no funds. The truly pioneering settlers had, however, arrived in 1853 and 1854, as stated above. Actually, all the settlers who arrived in 1857 were destitute; Tambs obtained work for them so that they survived the first winter. In a letter to A. C. Buchanan in 1858, Christopher Closter, then interpreter and emigrant agent with Buchanan in Quebec, informed his superior that there were twenty-five families totaling 126 persons in Bury. Closter learned that thirty in all of the approximately ninety original settlers in 1857 brought there by Tambs had been influenced to leave for the Western States, as they were dubbed, "by parties from the West." American agents represented a constant challenge; they could also hold out the anticipation of cheap or even free land. Closter complained about the forces that worked against Norwegian settlement in Canada. Closter was, however, happy to report that some of those who left for the United States had returned to the township and purchased land.

The following year, only fifteen families arriving from Norway moved into the eastern township; the remainder proceeded to the states. The settlement had started as a private undertaking and continued to be so; Closter's recommendation that the government "set apart a tract of land" for the Norwegians to encourage them to settle was never achieved. Because most of the settlers in Bury eventually moved to the Western States, Closter in his 1860 report described it as an unsuccessful settlement and noted that its failure was known in Norway, where it was "made use of to show that the cause of the unsuccessful settlement there is because of the unequal character of Canada to that of the Western States." Closter was by then engaged in promoting the Gaspé venture, described below, and some of those who left moved to Gaspé on Closter's encouragement.

Norwegians were still settling at least for some time before catching the "West fever" (*Vestfeber*), as it was called, and moving south. The Sherbrooke paper *Le Pionnier* reported on August 28, 1868, on Norwegian emigrants Quebec Province's solicitor general had sent to the Eastern Townships a few days earlier. The journal estimated there were roughly two hundred Norwegian emigrants, all guided by an agent toward the township of Ditton, which no longer exists; Ditton was located near Bury, where the Norwegian party was encouraged to take land. The newspaper described them as "good pioneers, able to adapt quickly to the climate of Canada, which is similar to that of their country." The history of the county has the following entry: "On August 25, 1868, sixteen families of Norwegians arrived [at Ditton]. Shortly after they got discouraged, and left one by one for the western states."

There remained a Norwegian presence in Bury in following decades, however. The eldest son of Tambs and his wife, Mary, another C. H. Tambs, served as secretary treasurer in Bury and is honored by having a street named after him. In 1876 Pastor Nils J. Ellestad of the Norwegian Synod formed a congregation in Bury with a membership of sixty-two that existed until 1884. Ellestad joined the clergy of the more moderate United Norwegian Lutheran Church when it was founded in 1890. In that decade a small congregation of the United Church offered its worship services to the community. Likely a continuation of the 1876 congregation, it had forty members in 1899 when its pastor, S. N. Garmoe, ended his work. The 1901 regional census lists the names of some eighty Norwegians in Bury; Anderson and Olson are by far the most common surnames. And, as Ulvestad claimed in the 1920s, "There are some Norwegian families there still."[14]

The Gaspé Peninsula

The village of Gaspé—located on Gaspé Basin at the tip of the Gaspé Peninsula or Gaspésie, which projects into the Gulf of St. Lawrence along the south shore of the St. Lawrence River in eastern Quebec Province—became the urban center of the best-known Norwegian colony at mid-century. In the early 1860s, Gaspé was a free port, and, as all foreign ships entering or leaving Canadian waters were required to stop there, no fewer than eleven nations established consulates on the shores of the bay. These were years of great economic development linked to international commerce. James John Lowndes, a prosperous businessman, served as vice consul for Sweden and Norway, a position frequently referred to as Norwegian consul due to the total dominance of Norwegian sailing ships in the traffic on the port.

Christopher Closter in his capacity as emigrant agent came to play a significant, perhaps decisive, role in the colony's annals. Ambitious and socially gifted, he was also described as "a slippery person," and questions about his reliability were raised early on. A. C. Buchanan felt, however, that Closter's services were essential when dealing with Norwegian settlers. In a report to Buchanan in December 1859, Closter recommended that the Canadian government "set apart three Townships for the exclusive settlement of Norwegians, in three different parts of Canada, namely, one on the borders of the Bay of Chaleur, one in the Eastern Townships, and one on the borders of Lake Huron."

Buchanan, encouraged by the early success of the Norwegian settlement in "the Eastern Section of the Province," expressed enthusiasm for the proposed colony on Chaleur Bay, whose northern shore is formed by the south shore of the Gaspé Peninsula. He praised "the hardy fishermen of Norway," whose fishing establishments in connection with settlement "would greatly conduce to the general prosperity of the country." Canadian authorities, eager to develop the remote part of the province, granted land for settlement. In 1860 the agricultural ministry reported that a Norwegian settlement was in progress at Malbay (Malbaie) township. Land within a stated area was intended for Norwegians only; each settler could select a hundred acres for a total price of twenty dollars over five years. It was a heavily wooded, isolated area with long and severe winters.[15]

The pioneer settlers at Gaspé were two brothers, Peter and Ludvig Brandt, from Trondheim who became fishermen in Lofoten. They emigrated in 1859

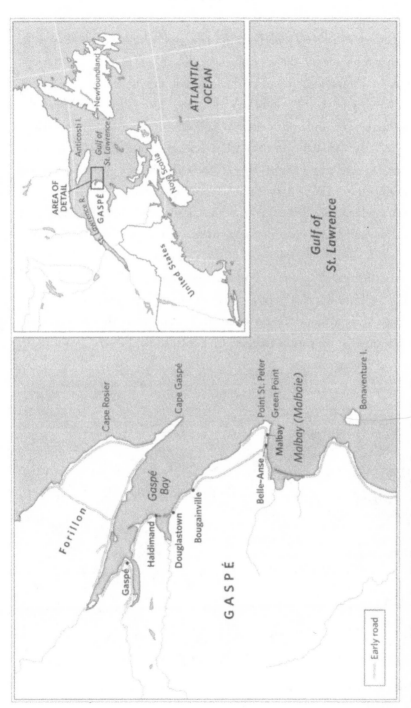

Pathways to Norwegian Settlements. 1860–63. *Drawn by Matt Kania*

to Montreal, where they found employment in the shipbuilding industry. In 1860 they responded to the government's offer of land and purchased property in Malbay. Their brother Fredrick Brandt and his family joined them from Norway in 1861. The brothers took land three miles inland from the coast, known as Corner-of-the-Beach (Coin-de-Banc), settling on the second range of lots. On August 1, 1860, Closter accompanied seven families who had arrived on the brig *Brødrene* from Trondheim; they traveled from Quebec by steamer to the Gaspé Basin with Closter as guide while they inspected the Crown lands and decided where to settle. Closter reported to Buchanan that he accompanied four men for twelve to fourteen days to inspect the land; they finally filed their application in the Office of the Crown Land for all the unsettled and unsold parcels in the township of Malbay.

The problem was that "not a single lot of land could be obtained from the Crown having footage on the seacoast." The land along the coast had been taken and settled, in part by Englishmen but chiefly by French Canadians. In

Corner-of-the-Beach (Coin-de-Banc), where Norwegians landed. *Photo by Odd S. Lovoll*

addition, there were no passable roads to the coast. All adult males, seventeen in all, were sent to Malbay to erect log houses on their respective lots. Peter and Ludvig built a large, seventeen-room log house on their heavily wooded land. When Fredrick and his family joined them in 1861, all three families lived together. Buchanan reported that, by the end of the year, "Nine families, have proceeded to settle in the District of Gaspé"—twenty-eight adults and twenty-two children. The Crown land agent at Gaspé, John Eden, commented favorably to Buchanan, stating, "You will be pleased to hear that the Norwegian settlers are making good progress, and appear to be perfectly satisfied with the lands they have taken for their settlement." Roads were also being built.

While progress was being made at Malbay and early outlooks seemed positive, Helge Haugan was sent to Norway in March 1860 by the provincial government as a recruitment agent; he promoted Gaspé by emphasizing its resemblance to Norway and its future prospects. He had also been instructed to recruit settlers for the Eastern Townships and the Ottawa district. In June 1861 Haugan left for Quebec on the ship *Flora*, which departed from Trondheim with 140 passengers from that port, the Lofoten islands, the Tromsø district, and points in Sweden. Many of the passengers disembarked when the ship stopped at Gaspé on its way to Quebec, and a number of them found their way to the Malbay settlement.

Following his visit to Gaspé, Closter was also sent to Norway as "further endeavor . . . to secure these valuable settlers." He returned to his native Stavanger, where in 1861 he brought out a revised edition of *Canada. En kortfattet skildring af dets geographiske beliggenhet* (Canada: A Brief Description of Its Geographical Location), which contained in condensed form important information about Canada and its lands and natural resources as well as practical details for the prospective settler. Closter returned with some seventy families from Stavanger and environs on the bark *Iris*, which departed on May 4, stopped at Grosse Île on July 10, and reached its final destination, Gaspé, on July 25. Closter informed chief emigration agent Buchanan that about four hundred Norwegian emigrants had settled in the district of

Gaspé. Buchanan in his report cites Closter as follows: "The greater part of those settled in Gaspé have taken up Crown lands in the townships of Malbay, Douglas, and Gaspé Bay South." Three areas of settlement thus existed by 1861.

N. C. Brun, a cousin of the Brandts, arrived in 1861 at the age of fifteen. He later became a prominent Lutheran pastor in the United States. In 1911 he contributed an article to the magazine *Symra* about his first years in Canada. The thirty families in Brun's settlement mostly had their roots in Trøndelag and North Norway and had not been swayed by Closter in their decision to emigrate. Brun offers the following observation about the arrival of the families from Stavanger: "The emigrants on this ship [*Iris*] were mainly from Stavanger; as they for the most part settled in the forests west of Gaspé, we rarely had contact with them. Their numbers were reckoned to be 70 families, and thus we were all in all about 100 Norwegian families. These families did not, however, live in a contiguous settlement, but were spread from 30 to 40 miles. Gaspé was regardless the capital for all of them."[16]

While in Stavanger, Closter had experienced strong opposition to his work as an emigrant agent for Canada, voiced most vigorously by the Lutheran minister Gustaf F. Dietrichson, who had returned there after a decade-long ministry to Norwegians in Wisconsin. In advance of his arrival, *Stavanger Amtstidende og Adresseavis*, the local newspaper, announced that in June 1858 Closter had been appointed "agent for the Norwegian and Swedish emigrants." Dietrichson challenged him "in a public forum at this place or in the newspapers to describe Canada's circumstances in general, and what there is that makes this land more than earlier suited for a place for Norwegians to emigrate." Closter's brother Asbjørn Kloster defended him in the press, stating that his book about Canada would soon be available, and privately encouraged the Gaspé project. Closter proceeded with his assignment, defended himself in the press, and even offered a lecture on conditions in Canada in Kloster's Quaker school. One might wonder if Dietrichson and *Stavanger Amtstidende og Adresseavis* harbored prejudice against individuals who had left the Lutheran state church. Dietrichson gave a blistering public lecture reprinted in

Amtstidende in which he accused Closter of giving incorrect description of conditions in Canada and persuading people "to give a promise to take residence at Gaspé." As circumstances developed, Dietrichson was correct in his warnings against settling at Gaspé, which he described as bleak, isolated, and heavily forested. Closter must nevertheless have had high hopes for Gaspé and gave evidence of his good faith by bringing his wife and family and other relatives to the settlement.

The settlers at Gaspé obviously had to make a living. As early as 1860 in a letter to Buchanan, Closter had requested assistance and aid as they adjusted to the new environment. The fact that they did not secure land along the shore was a significant problem; fishermen had huts on the beach where they lived when fishing. The cod fishing was at the time saturated by Jersey Island descendants. Norwegians engaged in cod fishing on their own and found employment with Jerseymen like Thomas Le Page, a prosperous pioneer settler in Bougainville, close to the Norwegian settlements. They did agricultural work and engaged in fishing, shipbuilding, and woodcutting for Le Page. Norwegians were also recruited to work in the salmon fisheries. Work for wages was difficult to find, but, as Brun recalls, the government came to their aid so that "every able-bodied man got all the work he could handle for a reasonable, daily wage." The Norwegian settlers became involved in building roads and bridges "through the almost impenetrable forest." In 1861 John Eden reported on "The Norwegians' Roads": two had been opened in the township of Malbay; they were twelve or fifteen feet wide and "fit to be travelled in wheeled vehicles." Older residents recall that in their youth a "Norwegian road" was still visible. "As soon as the roadwork was somewhat finished," Brun relates, "the work of clearing and building homes began."[17]

No Lutheran church existed to support the affiliation claimed by most of the settlers. The Closter family belonged to the Society of Friends and thus were independent in religious needs. The Lutheran settlers, however, sought clerical services at local Anglican and Methodist churches. Records from these churches give a glimpse into the lives of the Norwegian settlers. One finds that "due publication of Banns" bachelor Knud Arnesen and spinster

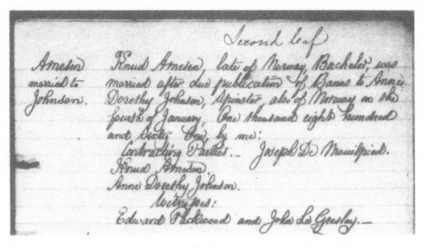

Because no local Lutheran church existed, Norwegian settlers sought clerical services in Anglican and Methodist congregations. The marriage listed in January 1861 was conducted in the Anglican church. *Quebec, Non-Catholic Parish Registers, 1763–1967*

Dorethy Johnson, late of Norway, were married in the Anglican church on January 4, 1861. There was also the burial of two-year-old Ellen Iversen. Several other burials were noted in the records, but there were also baptisms. On February 13, 1861, Anne Christine, daughter of Nelson Wold and wife Secelie Therese, both Norwegian, was baptized by the Methodist minister Isaac B. Stillman. Norwegians sought baptisms, marriages, and burials into 1863, giving evidence that there were some of their number living in the area at least until that year.

As noted above, a few Swedish emigrants got passage on Norwegian sailing ships. Carl Schöllström, soon Shieldstream, of Uppsala was a Swedish Quaker. He corresponded with Asbjørn Kloster. The first letter, dated May 22, 1861, informs Kloster that Shieldstream and his wife will the next day leave on the fine ship *Hermes* from Porsgrunn, Norway, for Boston and from there to St. John. Shieldstream was actually considering establishing a Quaker colony in North America for the fifty or so members of a Swedish Quaker Society. Kloster had sent him the Closter book on Canada, for which he offered thanks in the letter; its positive message had made him consider the possibility of relocating there. Shieldstream spent time at Gaspé and from there sent letters to Kloster. In one from March 15, 1862, he had clearly been convinced that Pastor Dietrichson was right in his admonition that no emigrant should be advised to go to Gaspé. The colony was failing. In his March letter to Kloster, Shieldstream accused Closter of being untruthful and unchristian. But in 1867, having moved to Norwich in the Province of Ontario, Shieldstream made conciliatory comments, stating that "I have nothing against him."

Closter has been greatly blamed for the colony's failure, but there were other causes as well. The colonists in the fall of 1861 were in great need and unable to obtain supplies for the coming winter. Much has been made of how Closter had collected most of the colonists' cash reserve and set off for Quebec to obtain desperately needed supplies. Brun recalls Closter "as he sat and stroked his long beautiful beard . . . and sought to convince my father to order provisions for the winter before it was too late." The rumor and later accusation was that Closter had used part of the money to pay off private debt; in one account of the situation Øverland assails him as a "faithless servant." What is clear is that when Closter landed with a boat and supplies at the Corner-of-the-Beach at the end of October, he had only part of what had been ordered. Brun's father had paid seventy dollars but received only provisions for twenty, which amounted to three barrels of flour, and a few pounds of butter, pork, coffee, and sugar. Brun laments that those who needed assistance most got the least.

The winter of 1861–62 was one of the coldest on record, and its privations killed the colony. On this background, Shieldstream launched his criticism of Closter. There were also voices that blamed the government, and with some justification. In a letter dated January 25, 1869, printed in the *Globe*, Henry Chesshyre, author of *Canada: Handbook for Emigrants*, accused the Canadian government of sinister motives in its eagerness to populate Lower Canada, as he referred to Quebec, when inducing the "people flocking from Norway" to settle on the coast of Gaspé. "Whilst the United States," Chesshyre continued, "receives the emigrant and takes care of him, the Canadian Government gives fair hopes, which the unfortunate find dashed to the ground on arrival at Quebec." One might of course question how fair Chesshyre's criticism is—Canadian government officials did better than he claims—but it is quite certain that the failure of the Gaspé project was not soon forgotten in Norway and had a chilling effect on future emigration to Canada.

Financial interests in the United States persisted in trying to attract emigrants. The Illinois Central Railroad in 1861, at the proposal of its agent in Sweden and Norway, Oscar Malmborg, sent agents to Quebec to meet arriving Norwegian and Swedish emigrants and convince them to come to the Middle West. The following summer, the Reverend Abraham Jacobson, a Norwegian American Lutheran minister in the Scandinavian Augustana Synod formed in 1860, was hired by the railroad to continue the work. The Central Railroad furnished him with five thousand circulars printed in Swedish on one side and Norwegian on the other. Jacobson relates how well he was received by the Episcopal bishop and ministers. He was authorized to be "a missionary to counsel Norwegian and Swedish immigrants in spiritual and temporal affairs. And during his four-month stay, he engaged in humanitarian and missionary work among the sick and needy. He visited Grosse Île once and Gaspé twice. Øverland in his account emphasizes that Jacobson's main mission, unknown to the Anglican clergy, was to persuade Norwegian emigrants to move to Illinois and purchase land from the railroad. The commission Jacobson's young synod got on land sales was an added motivation. As an authorized agent of the Illinois Central Railroad, Jacobson was expected to urge resettlement and was given the authority to issue necessary tickets.

Most Norwegians left the Gaspé settlement. The emigration report for 1862 conceded that "The Norwegian colony which the late Government tried to plant on the banks of St. Lawrence, has not succeeded so well." By autumn of that year, according to the report, of the three hundred Norwegian families there remained no more than ten. The reference to three hundred families seems overly high, based on earlier data. The report called unfounded "the charge of neglect, which has been brought against the [present] Government." Crown land agent John Eden faults the Norwegian settlers themselves for Gaspé's failure, claiming in an 1863 report that he "was greatly disappointed by the latest arrivals of Norwegian immigrants . . . they do not want to work, and are very dissatisfied at what has been done for them." He also made note of "some secret influence" that makes them discontented and tends to direct them to the West. Eden likely alludes to agents like the Reverend Jacobson, whose task it was to advance financial interests in the United States.

The most dramatic departure is described by Johan Schrøder, who relates how sixty Norwegian men and women without a penny to their names simply boarded a costal steamer in Gaspé in order to get to Quebec. When asked by the ticket taker to pay, they all refused. When reported to the captain, as Schrøder tells it, "he thought the trick the Norwegians had played on him was so grand that he burst out in a roar of laughter and took all of them along the four hundred miles to Quebec free, without charge, *and for nothing.*"[18]

WATERVILLE

Scandinavians settled with somewhat greater permanency in other parts of the province. One example, Waterville, is a small city of less than two thousand inhabitants located south of the city of Sherbrooke. It became a municipality only in 1876, but the history of its colonization dates back to the turn of the nineteenth century. Its cultural and demographic traditions relate to the coming of American New England, British United Kingdom, and French Quebec settlers. The arrival of Swedish and Norwegian emigrants contributed to the diversity of its demographic composition. Emigration to the region from the Nordic countries continued, but for most of them Canada became a corridor to the United States. The immigration agent L. Stafford reported for 1875 that the Norwegians and Swedes, with the exception of sixty-nine who remained in Canada, had come supplied with through tickets to the Western States. The Canadian government continued to pay the transportation cost for indigent emigrants to their destination in Canada if they intended to stay. This practice encouraged fraud. In 1879 the steamship *Circassian* of the Allan Line landed in Quebec on August 31 with 379 steerage emigrants, among them twenty Swedes. Using a fraudulent letter from the line's agent in Gothenburg, they tried to get the immigration agent to issue free tickets to Toronto. The agent became suspicious and, looking at the addresses on their luggage, discovered that most of them were headed for Michigan. One family of four settled in Waterville; the remaining sixteen paid their own way to the United States.

There was, as the 2001 history of Waterville claims, at that time an important Scandinavian population there. Carl O. Swanson came to Waterville from Sweden in 1869 at the age of twenty-five. He became the owner of a furniture factory two years later and engaged in attracting Swedish workers to his and other factories and farms in the area. He became a dominion immigration agent. In 1881 in Waterville the Canadian census lists ten Swedish-born heads of families, four Finnish, and one Norwegian, for a total of forty-five individuals.

The Norwegian emigration has an intriguing local connection in Norway. Knut Matsson Moene, wife Synneve, and three adult sons emigrated from the municipality of Ørsta in the Sunnmøre district on the country's northwest coast. They sailed from Liverpool on the steamship *Toronto* and disembarked in Quebec City on May 18, 1882. How they happened to settle in Waterville is not known, but the most likely scenario is that they were met by various agents, perhaps Swanson among them, and as cotters from Norway they might not have had resources to continue beyond Quebec at their own expense. Perhaps with Swanson's help, they likely took a river steamer to Montreal and from there went by train to Waterville. In following years others emigrated to Waterville from the same Norwegian community.

The Scandinavian, mainly Swedish and Norwegian, population apparently peaked in 1911 with 101 individuals; there are also much higher estimates, such as the claim in 1976 by the Reverend Carl Gustafson that around World War I there were "50 families with approximately 250 people all told." James

Knutson, a descendant of Knut and Synneve Moene and a resident of Waterville, tells the story of Swedeville, about a mile out of Waterville, where four Knutson families lived and operated a sawmill. Every piece of property was settled by Swedish and Norwegian families. Knutson in his memories of Swedeville concludes that "The Scandinavians are now gone . . . Entire families have moved on, mostly to Ontario and USA." Waterville had a similar loss of its Nordic citizens. At last count in 2014, only two dozen descendants of Scandinavian emigrants resided in Waterville and environs.[19]

Opportunities existed elsewhere. These were made known by settlers from the local community and were advertised in organized campaigns by provincial and state agencies and by private interests, such as railroad and colonization companies, and by other business concerns that would benefit financially from an expanding citizenry.

chapter 4

The American Campaign
for Settlers

*T*he Canadian gateway was a corridor to the United States for most Norwegian emigrants landing in the city of Quebec and other ports in Quebec Province after 1850. The final chapter will follow the emigrants on their route south and the hazards and the challenges they faced, including the sinking of the lake steamer *Atlantic.* The dramatic sailing of the Norwegian brig *Sleipner* from Bergen to Chicago is a part of the story of the corridor south from Quebec to the Upper Midwest. Advancement in rail connections created additional travel options.

The campaigns for immigrants by the states of Wisconsin, Minnesota, and Iowa are discussed individually; land-grant railroad companies played a significant role in the competition for immigrant settlers to the region. Chicago became the central point of a network of railroad lines. The early Norwegian settlements in east Texas became the destination for some. Among the Scandinavians in 1870, the Norwegian contingent outnumbered foreign-born Swedish and Danish settlers in the three states; however, the number of Swedish born in the United States was destined soon to exceed that of the Norwegians. The major areas of Norwegian settlement are delineated and in some cases illustrated by personal accounts of the journey to the region and settlement on the land.

THE DIARY OF MARTINIUS ANDREAS NORMANN

Martinius Andreas Normann was born in Tromsø, Norway, on December 8, 1838; his father was a successful merchant in that city. In 1864, at the age of twenty-six, Normann emigrated to North America, crossing the Atlantic on the bark *Bergen* with Captain P. Arnesen in command. It was one of two vessels that sailed north from Bergen to transport emigrants to Quebec from Tromsø that year; the other ship was the *Norge*, which left on April 24. Normann kept a daily record of his voyage from its beginning, when the *Bergen* departed from Tromsø on May 15. He traveled in cabin class and thus avoided the discomfort that steerage passengers endured. His diary is remarkably detailed, and throughout the voyage he makes insightful observations.

On Monday, June 27, after a voyage of some forty days or more, the bark anchored at Grosse Île, and the order was, "All hands on deck." The Norwegian flag was hoisted to give the nationality of the vessel. Then a doctor and interpreter, presumably the aforementioned Andrew Andersen, came on board and determined that all could proceed to Quebec. The interpreter handed out posters with Norwegian colors and text critical of the United States, concluding that "every emigrant who wanted to avoid misery should settle in Quebec Province or some other place in Canada, where we could count on help and high esteem." In his comments, Normann from time to time becomes class conscious and reveals his own privileged upbringing. The message spread by the Norwegian interpreter put many steerage passengers in a poor state of mind, he writes, "while the cabin passengers were more sensible and did not take notice of it."

They landed in the port of Quebec that evening. Customs people and yet another Norwegian interpreter met them. Their captain arranged transportation by a river steamer to Montreal. In the meantime, an agent offered a cheaper fare by rail, causing, as Normann writes, disorder among steerage emigrants, which was resolved amicably. Before stepping ashore, the emigrants bade a tearful good-bye to the crew and captain. Captain Arnesen was most helpful, accompanying the emigrants when they boarded the river steamer and escorting them to Montreal. Along the way, they passed many cities, among these "Kingston, one of the Englishmen's fortified cities." They all disembarked in Montreal. Normann mentions several Norwegians who came on board, among these a merchant named Christoffersen who invited him, Captain Arnesen, and two others on a tour of the city. Normann was impressed by the buildings in Montreal, especially the Catholic cathedral.

The steamer departed Montreal on July 3, traveling across a stormy Lake Ontario to Toronto. From there the emigrants would continue by rail. Certain railroad cars were, following inspection by some helpful Germans, found to have such poor quality that they were discarded. After the emigrants made many switches from unacceptable railroad cars to better ones, the train was ready to leave the station. "Fear and concern," Normann wrote, "was visible on the faces of the emigrants who earlier had not traveled by this means of transportation."

They came to a small town, Windsor, on the Detroit River and took a steam barge across to Detroit, arriving on July 4. Since the station staff was away celebrating Independence Day, the passengers had to take care of themselves and their luggage. In Detroit they boarded a train to Chicago, where they arrived July 6. There they were met by P. Hendriksen, a tailor, and others. The cabin passengers were entertained in Hendriksen's home. On July 14, Normann took the train to the town of Le Grand in northwestern Iowa. He continued to reside in Iowa; he had close contact with the Norwegian Synod and its educational institution Luther College in Decorah. In later entries he describes the people and circumstances he encounters.[1]

THE CORRIDOR SOUTH

A number of accounts of the journey from the port of Quebec to the United States have been recorded. The route changed over time, and there were alternative means of travel. Halle Steensland, a prominent businessman in Madison, Wisconsin, describes his journey in 1854; he left Stavanger on April 16 on the brig *Niord* and landed in Quebec six weeks later. The following is quoted from his reminiscences:

From Quebec the journey was by train to Montreal in Canada and from there by canal boat to Lake Ontario and across the lake on a steamship to Hamilton in Canada, from where we took the train to Windsor [Ontario] and then across the [Detroit] River to Detroit [Michigan] . . . At the railroad station we were put on a freight train with seats of planks—the soft side up, of course—without backs. Around us people were dying from cholera, which in 1854 was quite common, but as far as I can recall, our party reached unharmed the already then fairly famed Chicago.

A more systematic delineation of the changing avenues of transportation from Quebec to the United States can be made by consulting the annual reports of the chief emigration agent in Quebec during the years 1850 to 1864. The detailed information given in 1850, as well as in later reports, of "Routes, Distances and Rates of Passage, from Quebec" would help the emigrants make informed decisions and prevent them from being defrauded. In 1850 emigrants could go by steamer to Montreal, a trip lasting fourteen hours, with low deck fares, meaning the passengers remained on deck during the entire passage. There was strong competition between rail and steam companies for passengers. From Montreal emigrants could continue by rail to Buffalo, located on the shores of Lake Erie. Steamers left Buffalo for Milwaukee, Chicago, and other ports on Lake Michigan twice daily. The voyage through the Great Lakes could take from eight to ten days.

There was great improvement by 1853. Chief emigration agent Buchanan announced the opening of the Great Western Railway from the port of Hamilton on Lake Ontario to Detroit. A river steamer would take the emigrants to Hamilton from Quebec, the route Steensland described in 1854. From Detroit, they could board the Michigan Central Railroad to Chicago. Buchanan recommended this route because "all the dangerous navigation of Lake Erie is avoided." He further stated, "The distance from Quebec to Chicago by this route will be performed in comfortable steamers, and the remainder by railroad. Actual time of travel about 70 hours." The journey inland on special trains for emigrants might not have been as comfortable

There were special trains for the immigrants. From *The Story of American
Railroads* (1947)

as Buchanan's report outlines; Steensland's reminiscences suggest otherwise,
and similar complaints were not uncommon.

The Grand Trunk Railway system, with headquarters in Montreal, operated in the Canadian provinces of Quebec and Ontario as well as in New
England; by 1860 rails were completed from Quebec through to Sarnia on
Lake Huron and to Detroit. Emigrants could from there continue on to
Chicago on the Central Railroad, which took two days, or go by steamer
across the Great Lakes, a voyage of about one week. The lake passenger vessels were, Knut Gjerset writes, at mid-nineteenth century small propeller or
side-wheel steamers with crowded decks and small quarters.

The lake route was favored during the large immigration of the 1850s.
Traveling by steamboat on the rivers or Great Lakes was at that time fraught
with hazards of many kinds, including disaster at sea. One such tragic event
occurred in 1852, when the large Lake Erie steamer *Atlantic* on August 20
collided with another ship and sank; about five hundred people were on

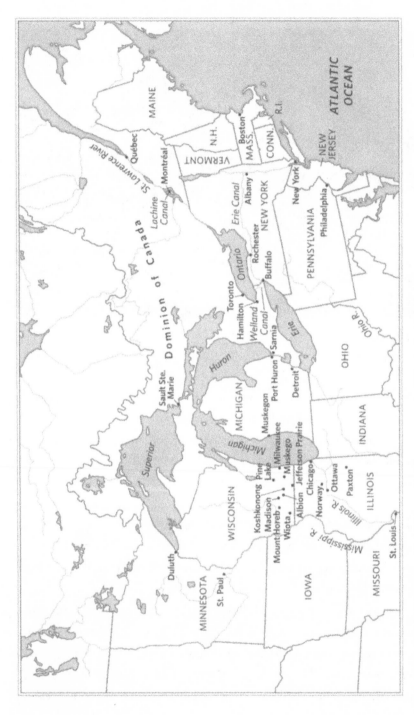

Immigration Destinations in the Upper Midwest, 1850–1875. *Drawn by Matt Kania*

board, mainly Norwegian and German emigrants. More than three hundred lives were lost, among these at least sixty-eight Norwegians, nearly all from Valdres. They had crossed the Atlantic on the bark *Argo* from Oslo to Quebec. A letter by one of the survivors, Erik Thorstad from Øyer in Gudbrandsdalen, describes the journey inland. He relates how their skipper, Captain R. Olsen, had accompanied them to Montreal. From there, by way of Toronto and Niagara Falls, they made it to Kingston, where they boarded a steamer to Buffalo. Many of the Norwegian emigrants were indigent, and "some seventy-five people from Valdres had free transportation" to Buffalo. They did not have enough money to pay passage across the lakes. In December, the consul for Sweden and Norway in Quebec sent the names of the *Argo*'s passengers who were saved because they could not embark on the Lake Erie steamer.

Thorstad relates how on board the *Atlantic* he made a bed of his chest, covered it with bedclothes, and went to sleep. "I awoke with a heavy shock," he wrote, and "Immediately suspecting that another boat had run into ours, I hastened up at once." The *Atlantic* had been rammed by the *Ogdensburg* and was quickly sinking. Thorstad was one of the sixty-four Norwegians rescued by being taken on board "the boat that had sunk ours." He concludes, "The misery and the cries of distress which I witnessed and heard that night are indescribable, and I shall not forget it all as long as I shall live." The surviving passengers were brought to Detroit by steamboat and continued from there by train to Chicago.[2]

Haldor Ostensen Rye from the farm Rye in Nord-Aurdal in Valdres was one of those surviving passengers. His oldest son, Osten, tells the story of the family's emigration and life in America. In the spring of 1852, as a debt-burdened man forced to sell his farm, Haldor Rye decided to emigrate to the Valdres settlement at Blue Mounds, Wisconsin. His brother Gullik Rye had made his home there the previous year. Haldor, as was the case in many instances, set out alone, planning to bring his wife, Guri Olsdatter Ragnus, and children over later. Indeed, Osten writes, "It was a stroke of luck that my father did not have enough money to bring his wife and three children with him," for they would then have been involved in the terrible tragedy on Lake Erie.

His father made it to Blue Mounds. "In the spring of 1853," Osten relates, "he was able to bring Mother and the children to this country with the exception of me, because I was the oldest of the children." Osten was yet not confirmed. In the spring of 1858 his father sent money for his ticket. Osten describes how he took farewell with "my dear birthplace Valdres" and then walked and ran to Lærdalsøra in Sogn and boarded a coastal steamer to Bergen. He traveled from Bergen on the sailing ship *Norman.* On June 24 he arrived at his parents' home in Adams, Green County, Wisconsin, where his father had purchased a small farm of eighty acres. They had by then Americanized the name Rye to Rear, and in America Osten Rye became Esten Rear. At the time he recorded the life stories of his father and mother, four brothers, five sisters, and himself, he had reached the age of eighty-two and was a resident of Fayette County, Iowa.[3]

DIRECT TO CHICAGO FROM NORWAY

On August 2, 1862, the Norwegian brig *Sleipner* tied up at the Galena railroad dock in the Chicago River harbor. It was welcomed with great fanfare, for it was indeed an unusual achievement and sight. The *Chicago Tribune* opined that "Possibly an arrival from the moon might have created more astonishment than the Norwegian built craft, with Norwegian captain and crew speaking a strange language, and crowded with light-haired Scandinavian farmers, their bouncing wives and children." There was a welcoming ceremony and an eight-gun salute involving the entire Chicago citizenry.

The *Sleipner* had left Bergen on May 23 with Captain H. J. Waage in command; it sailed by way of Quebec down the St. Lawrence River pulled by a steamer, through the Welland Canal, and then across the Great Lakes to Chicago. It transported 150 emigrants, forty of whom debarked in Detroit to continue to Chicago by rail. The *Sleipner* carried a cargo of salted herring, dried cod, and anchovies consigned to the wholesale firm of Svanøe and Synnestvedt in Chicago. Peter Svanøe, one of the two owners and, later, the

Plaque erected in Chicago to commemorate the centennial of the arrival of the brig *Sleipner*, on August 2, 1862. *Courtesy of Lawrence M. Nelson*

Swedish-Norwegian consul in Chicago, came from Bergen and had close ties to the commercial interests that had financed the expedition.

A small but growing Norwegian colony existed in Chicago in the 1860s; it numbered 8,325 by 1870, a fivefold increase from 1860. Norwegians in the city and beyond stood ready to consume familiar foodstuffs and buy other products from home. As return cargo, the ships could carry American grain and flour and other commodities. The success of the initial expedition encouraged the *Sleipner* to make additional crossings. And, though rural destinations were most common for Norwegian emigrants, urban stops increased in popularity as more emigrants came from Norway's cities. On the *Sleipner's* voyage to Chicago in the spring of 1864, craftsmen from Bergen who intended to settle in Chicago constituted most of the 144 emigrants on board.

The small vessel *Skjoldmøen* left on its hazardous America voyage from Bergen on April 12, 1863, and docked in Chicago on June 16. The *Chicago Tribune* was impressed to note that a ship only half the size of the largest river vessels had made it across the mighty Atlantic. In 1866 *Skandinaven* reported that the small brig *Vidar* "arrived in the capital of the West" on July 20, making the observation that "Norwegian hearts beat warmly for the dear old flag waving from the masthead." The arrival of these vessels represented contact with the homeland and strengthened a Norwegian American identity and enthusiasm. But with the *Vidar's* expedition to the interior of the American continent, this traffic apparently ceased. The reasons might be found in the stricter Norwegian regulations enacted in 1863 regarding the transport of passengers and goods on the same vessel, as well as, of course, in the displacement of Norwegian sailing vessels by steamships.

In 1860, in a population of 110,000, more than half of the citizens of Chicago were immigrants. A Norwegian colony may be dated from 1836; its few members resided in an area known as "the Sands," just north of the Chicago River where it empties into Lake Michigan. The Norwegian colony grew from 562 in 1850 to 1,313 ten years later and numbered in excess of 8,000 by 1870. Unsavory conditions in the original settlement inspired Norwegians to move west of the North Branch of the Chicago River. In the 1850s they increasingly congregated in the blocks around Milwaukee Avenue and Kinzie Street. Milwaukee Avenue was the central thoroughfare that provided members of the Norwegian community the route northwestward that they took in subsequent years. In the 1870s, Indiana Street (now Grand Avenue) a few blocks farther north became the center of the Norwegian enclave, referred to as Karl Johan, and Milwaukee Avenue became the center of the "Milwaukee Avenue" colony and beyond; the two streets were the Norwegians' promenades, "where they walked in their best clothes on Sundays and holidays." The fashionable Wicker Park neighborhood, where the more prosperous Norwegians resided, was developing. Because of the economic opportunities in a rapidly expanding urban economy, class differences among Norwegians were greater in Chicago than in other settlements.

Many of the Norwegians traveling to Chicago through Quebec arrived destitute. Poor people stranded in Quebec had for a time been sent to Chicago at the British emigration office's expense. As many as eight hundred assisted Norwegian emigrants arrived in 1854. Even emigrants with through tickets arrived penniless in Chicago, unable to proceed farther inland. In 1869 as many as 15,172 Norwegian and 24,260 Swedish emigrants arrived in Chicago, and most of them had run out of funds. In June 1866 the Scandinavian Emigrant Society was formed in order to "through combined forces . . . assist and protect our countrymen." One of the society's first acts was to help sixty Norwegians reach their destination in Wisconsin; dire poverty had stranded them for two weeks in the railroad depot.

The Norwegian colony in Chicago was nevertheless prospering. Notable individuals who settled there included Christopher Closter and his family. Helge A. Haugan, the son of agent Helge Haugan, moved to Chicago at the age of sixteen in 1863; there he with great success continued the gas-fitting and plumbing business he had learned when the Haugan family lived in Montreal. Haugan entered banking and became president of the State Bank of Chicago. Paul Steensland became one of the best-known businessmen and bankers in the community. Many of those who arrived in the 1850s and 1860s established businesses and made a living meeting the needs of the expanding Norwegian colony; they moved beyond its boundaries to achieve great financial success. The newspaper *Skandinaven* was founded in the Milwaukee Avenue colony in 1866 by John Anderson, who was born in Voss, Norway, in 1836 and came to Chicago with his parents in 1845. He succeeded in publishing and business, though he early on faced hardship as the family provider after the death of his father, Andrew, in 1849, when John was only thirteen. The first regular issue of *Skandinaven* was dated June 1, 1866. It was destined to become the largest Norwegian-language newspaper in the United States and, indeed, for some time the entire world. In the first issue, Anderson stated that the newspaper was a response to "a strong wish among Norwegians in Chicago to have a newspaper in the ancestral language here." He continued, "Many were completely convinced that Chicago was the place . . . the large central point for the prosperous Northwest where Scandinavians for the most part had settled."

Skandinaven published in its August 29, 1867, issue a list of eighty-one Norwegian and Danish businesses and professional people in Chicago, among them many successful men and women in the Norwegian colony. A number of these were building contractors. Great expansion in the building trades offered opportunities for Norwegian workers in occupations they favored, and they were rapidly drawn into the construction field. In Chicago's economic life, crafts as carpenters, painters, and other skilled and unskilled labor became a Norwegian, and in general a Scandinavian, niche. Increasing lake traffic led to crew, skippers, and also owners of lake vessels employing in 1860 one-fifth of the Norwegian male labor force. During the 1850s, domestic service gave employment to most women who worked outside the home. By the 1860s, however, women were entering other vocations within the Norwegian community itself, as dressmakers and even as midwives. Male tailors and shoemakers served the community, and there were Norwegian saloonkeepers and in 1860 one liquor merchant. By the late 1860s services and products, such as bakeries, butcher and sausage shops, watchmakers, and many others, were satisfied by people who made an appeal for business on the basis of nationality. Three Norwegian policemen patrolled the

Norwegian neighborhoods on the West Side in that decade. The community was maturing, and in a competitive multicultural environment it exhibited, in spite of inner disharmony and strife, ethnic identity and cohesion.[4]

THE COMPETITION FOR SETTLERS

The early official Canadian plans and efforts for Norwegian colonization in Canada largely failed. As historian Paul Gates points out, "The two chief difficulties which Canada was struggling against were the Canadian land system, which was less liberal than the American land system, and the attraction which the United States with its greater economic opportunities for labourers and capitalists had over the industrially backward country up north." The Gaspé project's failure caused distrust and served as a lesson for potential Norwegian settlers of the supposed perils and misfortunes associated with settlement in Canada. The provincial government, before confederation in 1867, did not, however, entirely abandon its efforts to attract immigrants to the province; to do so would leave the field to agents from other British colonies and American states, railroads, and land companies. Perhaps in self-defense against the foreign attacks on Canada as a field of immigration and as a response to demands from its own citizens, the government resumed its campaign to attract immigrants. The Province of Canada's focus was especially on Great Britain but also on Ireland and western Europe. Immediately after confederation, the Dominion of Canada and the four provinces of New Brunswick, Nova Scotia, Quebec, and Ontario together embarked upon an extensive campaign to secure for Canada a larger share of European emigration. The prairies stretching west of the province of Ontario toward the Rocky Mountains offered new attractions and opportunities for immigrants as well as for farmers south of the border; in 1870 "the prairies" were transferred to the Dominion. Not until the prairie provinces of the Canadian Northwest became the magnet, however, did Norwegians in the American Midwest and emigrants from Norway by the thousands feel impelled "to join hands with the pioneers of Canada in exploiting the rich resources."

Elias Stangeland, as agent in Quebec for the state of Wisconsin in 1854, met Norwegian sailing ships as they docked and gave passengers assistance in their continued travels, which one would expect he directed toward Wisconsin. In December of that year, however, the newspaper *Emigranten* carried an article titled "Emigration from Norway in 1854 and the State of Wisconsin's Emigrant Agent in Quebec," in which Stangeland was accused of neglecting his responsibilities. The purpose of his appointment would reasonably be, the article declared, "to make clear for all emigrants the advantages of settling in Wisconsin." The writer continued, "Had Mr. State Agent given his undivided activity to this cause, then the outcome would have been different and the State of Wisconsin would have had several hundred able families within its boundaries, who now have gone to Iowa and Minnesota." The reason for the poor performance, the writer claimed, was that Stangeland, in spite of being compensated for his services by the state of Wisconsin, persisted in his employment with the forwarding company Maxwell and Patten, which had been discredited by many Norwegians and for which *Emigranten* earlier had censured him.[5]

Wisconsin established the office of commissioner of immigration in 1852; the commissioner resided in New York. In his subsequent work he hired first a Norwegian and later two German assistants. All the northwestern states, especially after the Civil War, engaged in competition to attract immigrants to settle within their boundaries. Wisconsin took the lead in this effort. Advertising, as seen in the Canadian effort, was greatly employed, and not only by state governments but by steamship lines, land corporations, and railroad companies. Wisconsin's commissioner in New York distributed pamphlets in the German, Norwegian, and Dutch languages. The work continued the following years and also extended overseas. The office in 1854 appointed Stangeland as agent in Quebec for a period of six months; he is credited with directing most of the two thousand Norwegians who arrived there in the spring of that year to Wisconsin. Contrary to the appraisal made by the *Emigranten* piece, the commissioner deemed his work a success. Lack of funds, however, discontinued work at the Quebec agency at the end of the six months.

Chief recruitment efforts were confined to New York. In 1867 Wisconsin established a board of immigration; county committees were appointed with three members in each. The committees were to secure lists of friends and relatives of residents in their respective counties. In this way, a mailing list was created from which the board members sent pamphlets directly to individuals in the East and in Europe in such languages as Norwegian, Swedish, and German. These pamphlets reinforced the message of descriptive America letters sent from Norwegians in Wisconsin to kin in the old country.

The states sought people to settle and clear the land; workers were needed to build the railroads and do the hard jobs incident to pioneer life. The building of factories and towns and cities would follow. The result for the states was greater wealth, exploitation of resources, larger assessments, and greater investments in state improvement—all leading to prosperity and growth. Historian Theodore C. Blegen concludes that the campaigns of individual states not only brought within their state limits immigrants who would in any event have come west but also brought to America large numbers of immigrants who otherwise would likely not have left Europe.

Railways competed for the immigrant trade. Its capture meant success for the company: profitable traffic, the sale of railroad lands, the settlement of adjacent government land, and a labor supply. The Illinois Central Railroad was the first land-grant railroad; to aid in its construction it in 1851 received a grant of two and one half million acres of land in the eastern and central parts of Illinois. In order to settle the company's lands and build up traffic, the Central Railroad stationed emigration agents and runners in eastern port cities in the United States, sent agents to Norway, Sweden, and Germany, and, as has been noted, dispatched representatives to Quebec to induce people to go to Illinois and settle upon the railroad's lands. Swedish American Oscar Malmborg was selected to undertake the assignment in Sweden and Norway in 1854 and again in 1860. His modus operandi consisted of extensive travels throughout both countries; he distributed pamphlets in the two languages, inserted advertisements in urban and local newspapers using material furnished by the company, and visited people interested in emigration. Paul Gates concludes that the Illinois Central's activities did not produce a new movement and succeeded in diverting only a portion of the Scandinavian immigrants to eastern Illinois, a region that otherwise they would have neglected entirely. Nevertheless, Paxton, built on Illinois Central land grants, became a center for Swedish settlement in Illinois; the railroad's leadership negotiated with Swedish and Norwegian Lutheran leaders in the Scandinavian Augustana Synod in making it in 1863 the site of the Swedish Augustana College, founded in Chicago in 1860. The railroad thus received the Swedish Lutheran clergy's aid in attracting settlers; the church in return got a commission on land sales. Swedish emigrants were much more numerous in eastern Illinois than were Norwegians, but a handful of Norwegians were attracted from the great westward movement to settle there.

The Illinois Central's efforts are only one example of striving to promote and direct emigration to particular regions. As Gates reminds us, and as has been indicated earlier, Norway and Sweden and other northern European countries "became literally honeycombed with a hierarchy of emigration agents maintained by Canadian provinces and American states, railroads, and steamship companies."[6]

SETTLEMENT IN THE STATE OF WISCONSIN

Chicago was at mid-nineteenth century rapidly becoming the railroad capital of the nation. Between 1848, when the *Daily Democrat* proudly announced that ten miles of track had been laid on the Chicago and Galena Railroad, and 1856 Chicago became the center of a network of railroads connecting the Eastern Seaboard, the trans-Mississippi west, and all the larger cities in the Ohio and Mississippi valleys. All goods and passengers bound in either direction passed through the city.

Publicity campaigns were conducted both by railroad companies that simply wanted to transport settlers to the Midwest and by the land-grant railroads that in addition had acreage to sell. Wisconsin's land policy was a powerful inducement; lands granted to the state for school purposes were

Norwegian Settlements. *Drawn by Matt Kania*

offered for sale at extremely low prices, giving Wisconsin an advantage over its neighbor states in attracting immigrants. In 1871 the board of emigration was replaced by a commissioner of immigration appointed by the governor. The office was held for three years by Norwegian-born Ole C. Johnson; he was a hero of the Civil War, rose to the rank of colonel, and in 1863 succeeded Hans Christian Heg as the leader of the Fifteenth Wisconsin Regiment after Heg fell in the bloody battle at Chickamauga in northern Georgia in September of that year. In his first annual report in 1871, Johnson criticized the practice of many railroad and land companies, and even representatives of states, of giving glowing accounts of land in their states that "do not exist even in the imagination of the writer." He vowed to make a special effort to ensure that the information sent forth from his office would "be of the most reliable and trustworthy character," inviting potential settlers to place greater confidence in the information they received. In 1871 ten thousand pamphlets were published in Norwegian in Norway for distribution there and in Denmark. The practice had the advantage of the pamphlets being printed and distributed where they were certain to exert the most direct influence.

In his capacity as commissioner, Johnson engaged in close cooperation with the railroads, including the Chicago and Rock Island Railroad that in the spring of 1854 completed tracks to the east bank of the Mississippi River. The Milwaukee and St. Paul Railroad Company reached Prairie du Chien on the Mississippi in 1857; in 1873 it completed a line from Milwaukee south to Chicago. In 1858 the La Crosse and Milwaukee Railroad completed its line to La Crosse. A great number of railroad companies were established; their histories are complicated by mergers and name changes caused by consolidation with other lines and extensions to new regions. In his report for 1872, Johnson emphasizes the coming completion of new railroads, which he views as certain to be of great influence in the state's settlement. He also expresses hope for a road from the Mississippi to Lake Superior in the northwestern part of the state in order to open up a region that otherwise would remain a wilderness.[7]

Norwegian emigrants arriving in Wisconsin, whether coming through Quebec or New York, clearly had a number of decisions to make based on the information they received and the environment they encountered. The vast majority of newcomers during these years had landed in Quebec. A number of those who left the Gaspé colony initially settled in Wisconsin. In Eau Claire, Chippewa, and Dunn counties in northwestern Wisconsin, a large number of settlements were centered in the Chippewa Valley. The Brandts eventually settled there. Peter Brandt and Ludvig Brandt with their families abandoned Gaspé in the spring of 1862; Peter's and Brynhilde's daughter Amalia was born in Quebec in May and then baptized privately, as the baptismal certificate states, in the Anglican (Episcopal) church in Bury in August; there was consequently still a connecting link to the Bury Norwegian colony. Fredrick and his wife, Kjerstin, had a son in Malbay in August 1862, which delayed their departure. They all came to Dunn County and settled in the township of Colfax, where many Norwegians already lived. Peter farmed, Fredrick farmed and worked in a sawmill, and Ludvig was a carpenter.

Lumbering had attracted Norwegians to the Chippewa Valley as early as 1852, but the bulk arrived in the 1860s and later. They had mainly come from older settlements, demonstrating the pioneer settlers' prevalent restlessness. Better opportunities seemed always to be found by moving westward. The Brandts were also bitten by this bug, eventually moving to Acton township, south of Grove City in Meeker County, Minnesota. Acton had a growing settlement of emigrants from the Brandts' own Norwegian region of Trøndelag; the comfort of living among people from one's own locality, with a familiar dialect, memories, and traditions, became a powerful incentive in forming settlements of compatriots and might also have influenced the Brandts in their decision to move west.

The major areas of Norwegian settlement had been demarcated by the 1870s and have in the main persisted until the present time. One saga relates how the Theige family from Ringebu in the Gudbrandsdalen valley, Gulbrand and Karen and their six children, landed in Quebec on August 6, 1854, on

A Norwegian family harvests wheat in Dane County, Wisconsin, about 1875.
Photo by Andrew Dahl. Wisconsin Historical Society, WHi-1914

their way to Coon Valley in western Wisconsin. Norwegian settlement in Coon Valley and Coon Prairie in Vernon County began in 1848 with pioneer settlers from older settlements in the Muskego and Koshkonong regions. Thereafter came a rapid influx of Norwegians. The Theiges took the route over the Great Lakes to Milwaukee and then by railroad to Stoughton in Dane County, a town with a strongly marked Norwegian character located in an extensive area of rapidly increasing settlement. Gulbrand died of cholera after their arrival in Stoughton, as did their one-year-old son. Karen arrived in western Wisconsin in the fall of 1854 a widow with five children, the oldest, Ole, only seventeen. They settled on a quarter section of land on Coon Prairie.

Among foreign-born groups in Wisconsin, counting the immigrants and their American-born children, Norwegians were outnumbered only by the Germans. By 1870, as recorded in the federal census, Norwegians numbered close to 59,619, equal to 5.6 percent of the state's population of more than one million, a substantial increase from 9,467 in 1850, when the state had about 305,000 residents. During the pioneer era, Norwegian settlers continued to use wagons pulled by oxen, the so-called prairie schooners, even in regions where railroads had entered.

Norwegians settled in urban centers as well as in rural farming and lumbering regions of the state; they opened businesses or made a living as craftsmen and day laborers. In a lake city like Milwaukee, many men were employed as sailors. The possibility of employment as lumberjacks in the winter months often brought settlers to a particular region. The lumber camps in the vicinity of Eau Claire in west-central Minnesota attracted many Norwegian pioneers in the 1850s. The immigrant who began to cultivate the land faced great adjustment. American agriculture practices were very different from Norwegian traditions. While retaining many sociocultural traits, Norwegian farmers, like German and other Scandinavian immigrants, adjusted to the demands of new commercial methods of farming. A market economy replaced the self-sufficiency of the pioneer household.[8]

Minnesota's Campaign for Settlers

At mid-nineteenth century a great migration was in progress to the fields and forests of the Middle West by Americans and foreigners from the Atlantic states and immigrants from European shores. It was a rapid growth. In 1849, when Minnesota was made a territory, there were fewer than five thousand inhabitants. In 1860, two years after statehood and only ten years later, more than 172,000 had made the state their home.

Territories and states had a primary need for settlers in order to move forward in the cultivation of land; economic and social growth depended on it, as did the building of towns and transportation. The states of the Upper Midwest could all offer good farmland, and there were regions with large quantities of timber. A keen—and aggressive—competition for settlers was officially carried on by individual states; all agencies, public and private, that had something to gain by an influx of settlers participated in the campaign.

Wisconsin pioneered the official movement in 1852, as stated above; Minnesota followed the Wisconsin example, but not until March 1855, when the territorial legislature passed a measure for the governor to appoint an emigration commissioner to New York. That year there were forty thousand residents in the territory. The commissioner had the greatest success in attracting German settlers; he published articles about Minnesota in German and Belgian newspapers. The number of Germans grew in the decade after 1850 from 147 to 18,400, the latter equal to ten percent of Minnesota's total population that year. In an 1856 report to the legislature, the commissioner informed lawmakers that "During the present season, I sent a number of individuals to Minnesota, more or less able, some of whom were farmers, other mechanics . . . blacksmiths, carpenters, shoemakers, tanners, glovemakers, painters, lock and gunsmiths, and dressmakers." Land speculators and editors of the substantial number of newspapers published in Minnesota before 1855—often one and the same individual—had earlier brought the territory's advantages to the attention of outsiders and potential settlers.

The commissioner made little attempt to attract Scandinavians, though as early as 1853, with Wisconsin's vigorous efforts in mind, the desirability of Scandinavians as settlers had been emphasized. The federal census lists nine Norwegians in Minnesota in 1850; two of them were soldiers at Fort Snelling. That year the celebrated Swedish author Fredrika Bremer also visited Minnesota, making a strenuous journey from Chicago and finally by riverboat from Galena to St. Paul. There she stated her famous vision, "What a glorious new Scandinavia might not Minnesota become!" Her 1855 book *Homes of the New World,* translated also into Danish—the written standard in Norway as well—was an influential work, circulated widely in the Scandinavian countries and also in England and the United States. "The climate, the situation, the character of the scenery," Bremer concluded, "agrees with our people better than that of any other of the American States, and none of them appear to me to have a greater or more beautiful future before them than Minnesota."

The early 1850s introduced the first period of settlement in Minnesota. Beginning in 1851, parties of Norwegian settlers moved into western Houston and eastern Fillmore counties. Settlement expanded from the southeastern region of the territory west along the Iowa border. The Norwegian Spring Grove community in southern Houston County came to be a center in one of America's most densely populated Norwegian colonies; Spring Grove township served as an important distribution point for Norwegian settlement westward. Norwegian settlement to the north in Goodhue County commenced in 1854; the river town of Red Wing became an important marketplace. By 1857 there were 6,769 Norwegians in Minnesota, a total that increased to 11,893 by 1860. Much of the good land in Wisconsin was taken up by 1850, and as a result the attention of land seekers turned to Minnesota and Iowa.

Activity to attract settlers continued in 1858, during Minnesota's first year as a state. The agency in New York, however, was discontinued; during the following years pro-Minnesota propaganda intensified in newspapers and pamphlets. The pamphlet "Minnesota as a Home for Immigrants" was first published in 1864 in English, German, and Norwegian; the Norwegian copies were primarily intended for Scandinavians in America, and sources show that copies were sent to Norwegian settlements in Wisconsin.

No railroad was operated within the state until 1862. Before then immigrants could reach one of the points on the Mississippi that had rail connection east—Rock Island, Prairie du Chien, and La Crosse—and either take a steamboat to St. Paul or cross the river and reach their destination on foot or in ox-drawn wagons acquired at the river towns.

State activity reached its peak in 1867 with the creation of the board of immigration. Swedish immigrant Hans Mattson, a Civil War veteran and first secretary of the board, became a central figure in Minnesota's activities to attract Scandinavian settlers. The preceding year he had served as special immigration agent for Minnesota in Milwaukee and Chicago to advise Scandinavian immigrants; he also served as land agent for the St. Paul and Pacific Railway, the leading Scandinavian colonization railroad, until the spring of

1871. He related in his 1866 report that some twelve thousand Norwegian and Swedish immigrants reached the state that year. The Norwegians had come chiefly through Quebec and the Great Lakes to Milwaukee and Chicago and the Swedes via Liverpool, New York, and Chicago. As secretary, Mattson associated with board member Johan Schrøder. Minnesota stationed "'good, intelligent and honorable men of different nationalities' at the great immigration crossroads." They were appointed on the advice of their compatriots. Among the Norwegians was Thor K. Simmons, who in Norway had been a banker and who became the agent in Quebec. He first came to Dane County, Wisconsin, then to Red Wing, Minnesota, in 1856 as one of the earliest settlers; there he was a banker, wheat merchant, and county commissioner. K. Hasberg was appointed agent in Milwaukee and D. Wanvig in Trondheim.

The Civil War and the Dakota War slowed Norwegian settlement in the early 1860s, but it did not restrict Norwegian immigration to the state since most Norwegians entered by way of Quebec. By 1870 the immigrant and the second generation numbered 49,560, and only five years later, in 1875, there were 83,857 Norwegians in the state, equal to 14.08 percent of Minnesota's total population. The Homestead Act of 1862 made free fertile land available, and the land grants to the Pacific railways gave great impetus to the westward movement. The Northern Pacific Railway was the most important; in 1864 Congress gave the company nearly 40 million acres of land along its line from Lake Superior to Puget Sound. Construction began in northern Minnesota in 1870, and optimistically the two towns of Duluth and Superior were laid out. The line within Minnesota from Duluth to Moorhead was completed in December 1871.

The Northern Pacific was likely the most active of the railroad companies in cooperation with the state board; it carried out extensive campaigns by agents in the Scandinavian countries to attract the attention of prospective emigrants to Minnesota and the Dakotas. In spite of these efforts, there is, according to Carlton Qualey, little evidence to indicate that Norwegians settled to any extent on its lands in Minnesota. Through activity on the board of immigration, Mattson had worked to populate with Scandinavians the even-numbered sections, in other words, the government land, along the main line of the St. Paul and Pacific Railway; in 1868 as land agent for the St. Paul and Pacific, it was his assignment to settle the odd-numbered sections, the railroad's own land. In this connection Mattson visited Sweden in 1868 to recruit emigrants.

As the St. Paul and Pacific Railroad struck westward and northwestward, it located townsites at intervals of about eight miles; it reached Willmar in Kandiyohi County in 1869 and Benson in Swift County in the fall of 1870. The deliberate Scandinavian immigration policy enacted by the railroad company and also by the government explains the predominance of Norwegian and other Scandinavian settlers in the counties crossed by the St. Paul and Pacific. Existing settlements of Norwegians attracted other Norwegians; the railroad increased the attraction by cooperating with the Lutheran churches and providing free lots for church edifices. In December 1870 the Northern Pacific purchased the St. Paul and Pacific, and, since there was no change in the latter's administration, its land department continued the particularly Scandinavian propaganda along the main line from Meeker County westward. Norwegian American newspapers in 1871 still described the region as "the new Scandinavia."

In the summer of 1869, Norwegian-born newspaperman Paul Hjelm-Hansen traveled as a special agent of the state of Minnesota, riding an ox-drawn wagon from Alexandria in Douglas County to the Red River country. Hjelm-Hansen was fifty-seven when he emigrated in 1867. He returned to Alexandria after three weeks and wrote the first of fourteen promotional travel letters printed in *Nordisk Folkeblad.* Norwegian American newspapers recognized him as the discoverer of the Red River Valley for Scandinavian settlers. "In ten years," Hjelm-Hansen wrote, "this land will be built up and under cultivation, and will then become one of the richest and most beautiful regions in America. The soil is fertile to the highest degree and is exceptionally easy to cultivate, for there is not as much as a stone in the way of the plow." Hjelm-Hansen also described a healthy life in the wilderness: "On

Minnesota's high plains, I have become rid of my rheumatism, and in place of it, I have gained physical strength and a cheerful disposition." His assertion may be viewed as a response to the state's climate question, which became an issue in recruiting settlers. Defense of Minnesota's climate and rejection of the thought that the state was unfit for human habitation were apparent in the thousands of pamphlets that were distributed. The upper Red River Valley was destined to become one of the principal areas of Norwegian settlement in the Northwest.

Norwegian-born state senator Lars K. Aaker proposed to the governor the appointment of Hjelm-Hansen as special agent, which happened on June 5, 1869. Before doing so, Aaker called a meeting of the Scandinavian Emigrant Society of Minnesota, of which he was president, on March 16. The society was founded February 3, 1869; its purpose was "to promote emigration to the state and help distressed countrymen." The society's existence exemplified how state promotion of immigration fell under the auspices of the various ethnic groups. State efforts diminished as well because of the drive of the land-grant railroads and other private industries and persons who would benefit from the flow of immigration.[9]

Encouragement of Immigration in Iowa

According to historian Marcus Lee Hansen, the procession of immigrants steadily marching northward with "Bound for Minnesota" painted on their wagons became an unpleasant sight for many Iowans. Officially Iowa did little to attract immigrants compared to the efforts of its neighbors, Wisconsin and Minnesota. Iowa, raised to statehood in 1846, needed settlers, however, because an increase in population meant, as Hansen states, "more post offices and schools, better roads, a larger market, and the speedy arrival of the eagerly-desired railroad." But Hansen relates that the American-born Iowa residents from the New England and central states resisted recruitment of foreign-born settlers. As evidence, he contrasts the limited franchise accorded in the Iowa constitution with the liberal suffrage provisions for the foreign-born in Wisconsin and Minnesota. The Know-Nothing Party asserted its influence on party politics in the state as well. For whatever reason, the Iowa legislature was slow in enacting means to attract immigrants to the state.

However, immigrants became the only real source of new residents; migration could no longer be depended on as the eastern states became industrialized and movement west less attractive. Boosters in northern Iowa were especially anxious to have immigrants settle there, and in 1858 corporations and other business interests in Dubuque organized an emigrant association; a traveling agent was appointed to provide information about the advantages the state offered. As a consequence, though with much opposition, the legislature passed a law to station a commissioner of emigration in New York for two years. The Civil War, coming closely upon inauguration of the new policy, demanded new actions, however, and the office was discontinued. Regardless of policy, the number of immigrant residents rose, though Iowa was not receiving what might be seen as its fair share.

After the war, as people were needed to develop the great western prairies, many states were making plans to attract immigrants, and Iowa followed suit. In 1868 Mathias J. Rohlfs, a native of Germany, introduced a bill in the legislature to encourage immigration to the state. And in 1870 the Iowa legislature created a board of immigration composed of the governor and one member he appointed from each congressional district. The Reverend Claus L. Clausen, born in Denmark, was selected from the third district. He had in 1853 headed the St. Ansgar colonization project in northern Iowa. Germany, Holland, Scandinavia, and the eastern United States were accorded representation on the board. A pamphlet titled "Iowa: The Home of Immigrants," intended for wide distribution to encourage immigration, was published in 1869 in English, German, Dutch, Swedish, and Danish/Norwegian. From these regions it was hoped that new citizens could be secured.

Iowa's recruitment interests were closely intertwined with those of the railroad companies, which possessed vast stretches of land along their lines. Rock Island, just across from Davenport, Iowa, on the Mississippi, had a railroad connection to Chicago beginning in 1854. The railroads, which entered and expanded rapidly in the state in the following years, supported the board's work financially. The first railroad, launched in 1855, ran from Davenport westward to Iowa City. The result of the pamphlets, translated into select languages, and the agents sent to foreign countries was encouraging. By 1870 there were, according to the federal census, as many as 204,692 foreign-born settlers in the state. Immigrants had of course begun coming to Iowa much earlier, though their numbers remained small before the Civil War.

Beginning in the 1850s, the westward movement of Norwegian immigrants was directed especially into southern Minnesota and northern Iowa in advance of the railroad; the mother colonies were in most cases old settlements in Wisconsin. The movement into northeastern Iowa began in 1846 with the arrival of Ole Valle from the Koshkonong community, and the letters he sent back to Wisconsin opened the way to what became the state's main Norwegian area of settlement. The famous Washington Prairie colony in Winneshiek County was founded in 1850 by twelve families from Voss, Telemark, Sogn, and Valdres who had first stayed a few years in Wisconsin; Winneshiek County was to form a Norwegian center. The town of Decorah in time became the heart of the settlement in that part of the state, and indeed with Luther College established in 1862 it was an important cultural and religious center for Norwegians in America.

Direct emigration from Norway to Iowa began in 1853 when a large group from Toten chose Iowa instead of Texas, which had been the original plan. They landed in Quebec and made their way south, arriving in Clayton County, Iowa, on July 4. New Orleans and Galveston were the most common destinations for Norwegian sailing ships with emigrants to Texas, but a few intending to settle in the state sailed on vessels landing at Quebec City. In 1867, for instance, a party headed for east Texas landed in Quebec on the ship *Nor* from Oslo on July 14 and arrived in Texas the following month. Others made their way to the Lone Star State after first having settled in the Upper Midwest. The Norwegian colony in Bosque County northwest of Clifton, founded in 1854, became the most common destination.

Direct emigration to Iowa was encouraged by the railroad's completion later in the fifties. Norwegian settlement spread westward to the counties along the border with Minnesota, especially in Mitchell, Worth, and Winnebago. The two settlements in Story County, with Story City a focal point, date back to the mid-1850s, when two parties of colonists set out from the Fox River districts; they had both sent scouts to central Iowa prior to their move. The groups were separated along religious lines, although all of the colonists hailed from Sunnhordland. Those who formed the southern settlement in Story County had organized themselves as "Lutheran church people" into a congregation before they traveled west in ox-drawn covered wagons. A party of Haugeans formed a colony farther north. In this example, Lutheran divisions outweighed the strong bond of localism in the formation of settlements.

Migration increased as the railroad expanded throughout the state. For Norwegians who had settled in areas without railroad service, its arrival gave farmers easy access to markets and helped greatly in making the communities prosper. There was, however, steady movement from older communities as newcomers and members of younger generations set off for new areas of settlement. St. Ansgar in Mitchell County was founded by Pastor Clausen and two parties of some forty men traveling west from Wisconsin with ox teams and herds of cattle; they arrived at their claims in June 1853. The colony grew rapidly, and St. Ansgar became, to quote Qualey, "a dispersion point for Norwegian settlements in northern Iowa and southern Minnesota in the fifties and for northwestern Minnesota and the Dakotas later, especially after the arrival of the railroad in 1869."[10]

A CONCLUDING PERSPECTIVE

In 1870 the ethnic composition of Wisconsin and Minnesota showed a dominance of German settlers; counting only the foreign born, the German population numbered 152,804 in Wisconsin and 41,358 in Minnesota. Whereas Wisconsin had led in the number of Scandinavians in 1850, by 1870 the relative situation had changed so that Minnesota had 58,837 foreign-born Scandinavians compared to Wisconsin's 48,057. Norwegians were in both states the largest Scandinavian group. With 35,940 resident foreign-born

Norwegians in Minnesota, there were in the state 20,937 Swedes and 1,910 Danes. The same year Wisconsin counted 40,046 Norwegians, 5,212 Danes, and 2,799 Swedes. There were 16,029 Norwegian-born Iowans in 1870, an increase from 5,353 only ten years earlier; Germans numbered 65,957.

The Northern Pacific line was completed from Lake Superior to Moorhead on the Red River on December 12, 1871; from there it entered Dakota Territory and reached Jamestown in 1872 and Bismarck the following year. From August 1871 to April 1873, the company produced a promotional four-page monthly titled *Land and Emigration*, which was published in London and distributed by some 116 agents in Great Britain. It was thus used exclusively to acquaint people in the British Isles with the company and its vast land holdings, encourage them to emigrate to America, and convince them of the benefits of settling along its line. The company in its recruitment, at least as judged by the monthly's content, appeared to ignore the two populations that in time would become the most visible in North Dakota, the Russian-Germans and the Norwegians.

The move into Dakota Territory meant an adjustment to the prairie landscape. Norwegians preferred regions with forest land, but such terrain became difficult to find; the great plains to the west awaited settlement. Along the rivers where many Norwegians settled were trees that could be used for building material. In 1889 the territory became the two states North Dakota and South Dakota. Many Norwegians settled both south and north in the years after the Civil War, but the great land boom of the 1880s saw a much larger stream into the region. The acceleration of Norwegian settlement was caused by a series of wet years but also by the expansion of the railroad and, as in the other states in the Upper Midwest, by public campaigns made by the territorial immigration commission, land companies, newspapers, and personal correspondence from settlers in the region. By 1900 South Dakota had 18,602 Norwegian born and North Dakota 29,295; the latter state held in terms of percentage the honor of being the most Norwegian in the Union.

The timeline of the historical narrative makes the two Dakotas less immediate to the theme of the Canadian gateway than regions to the east, but not for the most part different. Many of those who moved to either South Dakota or North Dakota from settlements farther east had originally landed in Quebec. A manuscript autobiography by Erick J. Berdahl, written about 1928, makes that point. Berdahl was born in Sogn, Norway, on August 8, 1850. His parents, Johannes and Kristi Berdahl, made a scant living on a small rented place called Jordahl on the Sognefjord with no connecting roads.

Earlier emigrants from the community, having settled in Iowa, sent back good tidings about the new country. During the spring of 1856, people made plans to join their former neighbors in Winneshiek County, and Erick's father wanted to be one of them, but he had no means to bring his family of six across the Atlantic and to Iowa. The issue was settled when one of the emigrants advanced him money that would be repaid after settling in America.

The emigrants left from Bergen on the sailing ship *Columbus;* Erick at age six did not recall much from the nine-week-long crossing to Quebec but assumed it must have been a tedious ride. It took them another three weeks to reach Winneshiek County. Johannes at first made a living at menial labor, grubbing and harvesting hay. Newcomers regularly provided cheap labor. The first winter he worked in timber and splitting rail. After four years in northeastern Iowa, the family made plans to move to Minnesota. In 1860 they settled on a school section in Spring Grove in Houston County. In the meantime, a child had been born. New neighbors helped them, and the arduous task of clearing land began.

Erick shares memories from "the dreadful Period" of the Civil War. In 1864 his father bought eighty acres of prairie land south of the school land, a plot he thought would be easier to clear. In the spring of 1865 they moved to a dugout on their new land; there were by then seven children in the family. Their pastor was the Reverend Clausen. Erick was confirmed in 1864.

The Berdahl family typified constant movement westward and became pioneer settlers more than once. With a growing family—a total of nine children by 1867—Johannes looked for a larger farm. Selling the eighty acres and the improvements on the school land enabled the family to purchase a quarter section of land in Fillmore County; they moved into a small log cabin. Their first harvest at the new place was done by a McCormick reaper pulled by four horses, a great improvement over previous techniques, but the hay was still cut with a scythe. In cooperation with Norwegian neighbors, the Berdahls purchased a thresher. The family was clearly moving forward financially. The oldest children were by then at an age where their labor became a significant asset, but, too, they soon would leave home.

Apparently the wish to find abundant adjacent land for all family members made Johannes look farther west. With a couple of neighbors, in the spring of 1871 he went as far as the Sioux River; there they found land and timber that suited them. The following spring, traveling west with two pairs of horses and covered rigs, Berdahl family members visited Sioux Falls. Together with an agent they explored land along Slip Up Creek. They decided on a parcel farther north, close to timber and the Norwegian settlement along the Sioux River. They filed their claims properly.

The move to Dakota began on May 18, 1873; the caravan moving westward included families in addition to their own. They could transport goods part of the way by train, but otherwise their loaded rigs were pulled by oxen and horses; their cattle, colts, and sheep followed the wagons. After four weeks with many struggles, they caught sight of Slip Up Valley. Johannes had gone ahead of them and built a dugout on their homestead, which, as Erick writes, gave the family a place to crawl into. The Slip Up Creek settlement grew and prospered. Eric continues his autobiographical account with his own marriage, children, and livelihood. As a concluding example, the story of the Berdahl family captures the shared humanity and drama of the immigrant experience. It becomes in addition a perspective on the fundamental thread of the present study.[11]

Epilogue

The Canadian national household survey for 2011 showed that 452,705 Canadians identified themselves as Norwegian, having either multiple or single ethnic origin; 44,075 identified themselves as single-ethnic Norwegian. Norwegians constituted the largest Scandinavian ethnic group. Clearly, the Canadian gateway was entered by Norwegians after the final, 1874 voyage of sailing ships carrying emigrants.

Canada was no longer mainly a corridor south but a final destination for many emigrating Norwegians. The home country's statistics record emigration to Canada beginning in 1886, although individual emigrants, as shown in the Waterville settlement and also suggested elsewhere in the text, arrived earlier and found their home in Canada. According to the official data, between 1886 and 1930, a total of 38,661 Norwegians had Canada as their final destination; 54 percent emigrated in the decade of the 1920s, in part due to restrictions on immigration to the United States. Only 783 Norwegians are listed as moving to Canada between 1886 and 1900. In order to get a complete picture, the much larger stream of Norwegians north from the United States must be added.

A scholarly treatment of Norwegian immigration to and settlement in Canada awaits the interested historian and is much desired. Adding in the Canadian historical experience will complete the history of Norwegian immigration to North America.

The three prairie provinces—Manitoba, Saskatchewan, and Alberta—
became magnets for land-seeking emigrants directly from Norway and for
those migrating across the Dominion of Canada's southern border. The
Dominion's department of immigration and colonization conducted an
aggressive campaign to encourage farmers and young farm workers to emigrate from Europe. Canada's land act made homesteads available as early as
1872, two years after the prairie provinces were transferred to the Dominion.
The Canadian government, in Norwegian and other Scandinavian newspapers, advertised the advantages of settling there; special emigration and transportation agents distributed pamphlets in Norwegian. "Fertile Homesteads
Free for All in the Canadian Northwest," the propaganda promised.

The building of the Canadian Pacific Railway, beginning in 1881, opened
up the Canadian Northwest for settlement. It reached British Columbia in
1885, geographically unifying Canada. Beginning in 1903, the railway company
operated the Canadian Pacific Line, with steamship connection from Liverpool to Quebec and St. John. Its chief agent in Stavanger, Joh. G. Sandsmark,
explained how comfortable the line's steamships were, even for passengers
traveling third class; in transit in Liverpool the emigrants could find lodging
at the line's hotel, the Boston. Arriving in a Canadian port city, the emigrants
could continue their journey on the Canadian Pacific Railway to western
Canada.

As in the United States, the Dominion granted land tracts on either side
of the rail line and reserved alternate sections for homestead and preemption
purposes, with some flexibility. The Canadian Pacific and the Dominion
sought settlers from the United States. Agents stationed in upper midwestern cities offered free homesteads and free transportation for those who
wished to inspect land in the Canadian prairie provinces. A rural depression
in the Midwest beginning in the mid-1880s and the agricultural crises after
1893 made opportunities farther north appealing to farm laborers and tenant
farmers. Land for the next generation was lacking in many parts of the Midwest. Year after year, the Dominion distributed pamphlets in the United States
that bore the title "The Last Best West," suggesting that the Canadian prairie

constituted a natural extension of the Dakotas and beyond. The frontier experience could for many be repeated farther north and west.

The ascendancy of Canada's western provinces was based on access to abundant free and inexpensive land and transportation. The coming of Nordic immigrants as well as migrants from the Midwest gave impetus to a growing prosperity. Most of the Norwegians arriving directly from the homeland after 1885 made their new homes in the Canadian Northwest. Between 1893 and 1914, as many as 98,000 Scandinavian Americans took land in the three prairie provinces; some 55,000 were of Norwegian origin. During these years, an increase in wheat prices and a decline in transportation costs produced an economic boom. The single-nationality immigrant colonies prospered. It was, to quote historian Robert England, "Canada's experiment in nation building"; names such as New Iceland, New Norway, and New Sweden identified the nationality of many of these colonies. A cross-border relationship was established and has continued up to the present time.[1]

Acknowledgments

The assistance of many people and institutions made the extensive fieldwork and research this study required both enjoyable and successful. I was received with warmth and interest wherever I went. I give my deeply felt thanks to all. Regretfully, I cannot list the names of everyone who in one way or another showed interest in and promoted the project.

During my five weeks of fieldwork in Norway, a number of people engaged themselves in my research. Hans Eirik Aarek was my guide at the Quaker archives at the Regional State Archives in Stavanger. In Bergen, I thank Yngve Nedrebø at the Regional State Archives for his help. Roger Kvarsvik at the Maritime Museum in Bergen deserves a special shout-out for his persistent interest in and contributions to the research. In Oslo, the staff at the National Archives and the Regional State Archives patiently searched for requested documents, as did Lisa Benson at the Norwegian Maritime Museum and Espen Søbye at the National Bureau of Statistics. Much research time was spent at the National Library of Norway. Everyone was most helpful, but I would like especially to express my gratitude to Michelle Tisdel, Jana Sverdljuk Bentze, and Dina Tolfsby. Longtime friend and former research assistant Jostein Molde shared his work on emigration from Trøndelag and introduced me to Donna and John Haines and Susan Haines Ruchie, who gave me much information about their family's Gaspé colony history. Lise Løken and Henry Hansen and May Lunde advanced my research as well. I thank them most sincerely. I also wish to thank Terje Mikael Hasle Joranger for his help and encouragement. Fredrik Bochelie gave me a copy of a diary in his possession; a portion of it is printed in the present study.

Gary Erickson presented the project in *Norwegian American Weekly*, editor Amy Boxrud in *Sons of Norway Viking*, Jackie Henry in the Norwegian-American Historical Association (NAHA) newsletter, and editor Maria Vang Ormhaug in *Norwegians Worldwide*. These presentations encouraged many people to send in family histories relating to arrivals in Quebec. Professor Solveig Zempel solicited family histories. A selection of these historical accounts is included in the book. All personal narratives will be stored in the NAHA archives. I thank NAHA archivist Jeff Sauve and the staff at the Rolvaag Memorial Library at St. Olaf College for their friendly and patient assistance; a special thanks to Kasia Gonnerman and Ken Johnson. Professor Mary Cisar was my generous French-English translator. Former research assistant Aaron Hanson supplied information. James Berdahl forwarded a diary and other information about the Berdahl family; part of the diary is featured. Deborah Miller at the Minnesota Historical Society responded consistently to my queries.

I owe a debt of thanks to the many people who promoted my research in the course of five different excursions to Quebec and Ontario. I received excellent and professional help at the Library and Archives Canada in Ottawa; among the many librarians who gave of their time I should especially like to recognize reference librarian Gaya Déry. During my two visits to Quebec City, I was cordially received at the Naval Museum, the Museums of Civilization, and the Port Authority of Quebec; customs officers, most especially Patrick Lamontagne, gave me insight into how traffic to the port was observed and regulated. Guides at Grosse Île responded with much interest and patience to my many queries. In Montreal and the Eastern Townships in Quebec Province my enthusiastic and knowledgeable guide was James Knutson. He gave invaluable assistance in my research on Norwegian settlements in Bury and Waterville. Wendy Olson was a contact person in Bury. In Sherbrooke I was warmly welcomed and assisted in my research at the

History Society of Sherbrooke and at Bishop's University in Lennoxville. In Montreal I should especially like to thank Eric Major at the Montreal Archeology and History Complex, Carolyn Osborne at the Mariner's House of Montreal, and Jason Zuidema at the North American Maritime Ministry Association. Members of the Montreal Norwegian Club were inspiring contacts, most especially Ellen Laughlin and Marie Blydt-Hansen.

On Gaspé no one more consistently or enthusiastically assisted in my research than Martha Costello in Manotick, Ontario; I extend special appreciation to her. Professor Judith Fingard in Halifax, Nova Scotia, was a valuable and friendly resource person and responded to my queries with great insight. At the Musée de la Gaspésie in Gaspé archivist Jeannot Bourdages and curator Félix Fournier were most helpful. I also thank Professor Jean-Marie Thibeault. Wendy Le Marquand for an entire day became my guide to the locations of the Norwegian colonies in the Malbay district.

A special word of gratitude goes to Professor Emeritus Lars Erik Larson, University of Wisconsin–Whitewater. Learning of my interest and research in Norwegian emigration to Canada 1850 to 1874, a topic he himself has studied, he most generously offered to send me his files. These helped me plan my own research, even when duplicating our paths, and provided valuable source material. Professor Larson's files along with my own will find a permanent home in the NAHA archives. Derwood Johnson of Waco, Texas, provided information on Norwegians in Texas. I extend my sincere thanks to Matt Kania, Matt Hero, Inc., Duluth, Minnesota, for the six maps he created.

It was a pleasure to again work with editor Shannon Pennefeather on preparing the manuscript for publication.

Notes

Notes to Chapter 1

1. Jacob S. Worm-Müller, "Navigasjonsaktens ophævelse og frihandelens seier," in Fredrik Scheel and Jacob S. Worm-Müller, eds., *Den norske sjøfarts historie fra de ældste tider til vore dage* (Oslo: Steenske forlag, 1935), 2:235.

2. Robert Bothwell, *The Penguin History of Canada* (Toronto: Penguin Canada, 2007), 8–9; Sean T. Cadigan, *Newfoundland and Labrador: A History* (Toronto: University of Toronto Press, 2009), 26–30. See Birgitta Linderoth Wallace, *Westward Vikings: The Saga of L'Anse aux Meadows* (St. John's, Newfoundland: Historic Sites Association of Newfoundland and Labrador, 2006).

3. Jacques Lacoursière and Robin Philpot, *A People's History of Quebec* (Montreal: Baraka Books, 2009), 9–11, quote 9; Paul-André Linteau, *The History of Montréal: The Story of a Great North American City*, trans. Peter McCambridge (Montreal: Baraka Books, 2013), 15–16, 17–18; Bothwell, *Penguin History of Canada*, 15, 19, 29; Gilbert Parker and Claude G. Bryan, *Old Quebec: The Fortress of New France* (London: Macmillan and Co., Ltd, 1903; Nabu Public Domains Reprints), 4–12.

A cross was raised in the port city of Gaspé in 1934 to commemorate the four-hundredth anniversary of the erection of the initial cross and the beginnings of New France.

4. Parker and Bryan, *Old Quebec*, xx, 19, 42, 183–84; Serge Bernier, et al., *Military History of Quebec City, 1608–2008* (Montreal: Art Global, 2008), 17–18, 55, quote 18, 55.

5. Bothwell, *Penguin History of Canada*, 53–54, quote 53; Lacoursière and Philpot, *People's History of Quebec*, 14, 53–54; Margaret Conrad, *A Concise History of Canada* (Cambridge: Cambridge University Press, 2012), 74–75; Yves Frenette, *The Anglo-Normans in Eastern Canada*, Canada's Ethnic Group Series 21 (Ottawa: Canadian Historical

Association, 1996). See Rosemary E. Ommer, *From Outpost to Outport: A Structural Analysis of the Jersey-Gaspé Cod Fishery, 1767–1886* (Montreal and Kingston: McGill-Queen's University Press, 1991).

Félix Fournier, conservateur, Musée de la Gaspésie, provided the booklet. Many of the expelled Acadians later settled in Louisiana, where they became known as Cajuns.

6. Bothwell, *Penguin History of Canada*, 68–70, 74, 75–76, 82, 87–89, 128–29; Lacoursière and Philpot, *People's History of Quebec*, 35, 43, 51–52, 71, 73–74, quote 71; Parker and Bryan, *Old Quebec*, 182–84; Conrad, *Concise History of Canada*, 74, 75–79; Bernier, *Military History of Quebec City*, 105–16, quote 55; Peter N. Moogh, *La Nouvelle France: The Making of French Canada—A Cultural History* (East Lansing: Michigan State University Press, 2000), 272–73, quote 273.

In 1800 Spain returned its portion to France, which in 1803 sold it to the United States. With the Louisiana Purchase in 1803, the United States gained approximately 828 million square miles of territory, thereby doubling the size of the young republic.

7. Robert Middlekauff, *The Glorious Cause: The American Revolution 1763–1769* (New York: Oxford University Press, 1982), 266–73 328, 570–71, 575; Bothwell, *Penguin History of Canada*, 118–19, quote 119; Conrad, *Concise History of Canada*, 95–96.

8. Bothwell, *Penguin History of Canada*, 134–35; Stanley C. Johnson, *A History of Emigration from the United Kingdom to North America, 1763–1912* (London: Frank Cass and Co., 1966), 191–93, 211–16.

9. Bothwell, *Penguin History of Canada*, 138–47, 151–52, 167–68, 186, quote 196; Conrad, *Concise History of Canada*, 122–27; Linteau, *History of Montreal*, 76–81; Donald Hartman Akenson, *The Irish in Ontario: A Study in Rural History*, 2nd ed. (Montreal: McGill-Queen's University Press, 1999), 16–20.

10. Conrad, *Concise History of Canada*, 147–52, quote 150; Bothwell, *Penguin History of Canada*, 210–13; Lacoursière and Philpot, *People's History of Quebec*, 115; Desmond Morton, *A Short History of Canada* (Toronto: McClelland and Stewart, Ltd., 2006), 88–98, quote 11.

11. Ingrid Semmingsen, *Veien mot vest. Utvandringen fra Norge til Amerika 1825–1865* (Oslo: H. Aschehoug and Co. [W. Nygaard], 1941), 14–24; Theodore C. Blegen, *Norwegian Migration to America, 1825–1860* (Northfield, MN: Norwegian-American Historical Association (hereafter, NAHA), 1931), 41–42, 49–50, quote 19; National Archives, Prerogative Court of Canterbury and related Probate Jurisdiction, Will Registers, Webster Quire Numbers: 95–143, 1781 (Prob 11/1075); Odd S. Lovoll, *A Century of Urban Life: The Norwegians in Chicago before 1930* (Northfield, MN: NAHA,

1988), 9, 11; Maldvyn Allen Jones, *American Immigration* (Chicago: University of Chicago Press, 1967), 64–66, 92–116, quote 92. I thank Ola Teige, postdoctoral research fellow (history), for the information on Cornelius Wilson. See John O. Evjen, *Scandinavian Immigrants in New York, 1630–1674* (Minneapolis, MN: K. C. Holter Publishing Company, 1916).

12. Blegen, *Norwegian Migration* (1931), 17, 75; George Richardson, *Rise and Progress of the Society of Friends in Norway* (London: Charles Gilpin, 1849), ix–xi, 8, 16, 25–27, 30, 34, 44, 47, 87–88, quotes ix, 16, 87; Andreas Seierstad, *Kyrkjelegt Reformarbeid i Norig i Nittande Hundreaaret* (Bergen, Norway: A/S Lunde and Co. Forlag, 1925), 167–97, 210–223, 234, 334–35. See also Henry J. Cadbury, "The Norwegian Quakers of 1825," *Norwegian-American Studies and Records* 1 (1926): 60–94. See the article by Hans Eirik Aarek, "A Short History of the Troms Quakers and Their Emigration to America," *Norwegian-American Studies* 35 (2000): 91–140.

13. Odd S. Lovoll, *The Promise of America: A History of the Norwegian-American People*, rev. ed. (Minneapolis: University of Minnesota Press, 1999), 44–46; Blegen, *Norwegian Migration* (1931), 24–25, 27–31, 39, 58. Lars Larsen (Geilane)'s farm name is identified in parentheses.

14. Jacob S. Worm-Müller and Fredrik Scheel, eds., *Den norske sjøfarts historie fra de ældste tider til vore dage* (Oslo: Steenske forlag, 1951), 2:547–48, 550; Theodore C. Blegen, ed., *Land of Their Choice: The Immigrants Write Home* (Minneapolis: University of Minnesota Press, 1955), quotes 25, 45; Blegen, *Norwegian Migration* (1931), 61–66; Carlton C. Qualey, *Norwegian Settlement in the United States* (Northfield, MN: NAHA, 1938), 22, 25–32, 26, 29–30; Knud Langeland, *Norwegians in America: Some Records of the Norwegian Emigration to America*, trans. Odd-Steinar Dybvad Raneng (Waukon, IA: Astri My Astri Publishing, 2012), 20.

15. Jeff M. Sauve, "From Norway to Quebec," *Sons of Norway Viking* 5 (2013): 9; Gary Krahenbuhl of Tempe, Arizona, provided information on the Espe family, including two booklets he authored: *Guri Bly* and *Traveling West in the Search for Gold in 1859.*

16. Blegen, *Norwegian Migration* (1931), 75, 81, 88–9, 91, 95–102, quotes 75, 81; Qualey, *Norwegian Settlement*, 27–28, 29–30, 41, 44, quote 43; Lovoll, *A Century of Urban Life*, 11–12; Lovoll, *Promise of America*, 13–16, 46–47, 51–54; Knud Langeland, *Nordmændene i Amerika. Nogle Optegnelser om norsk Udvandring til Amerika* (Chicago: John Anderson and Co., 1888), 26–31, 33–36. See also Henry J. Cadbury, "Four Immigrant Shiploads of 1836 and 1837," *Norwegian-American Studies and Records* 2 (1927): 20–52. Ole Knudsen Nattestad, *Beskrivelse over en Reise til Nordamerica begyndt den 8de April 1837 og skrevet paa*

Skibet Hilda *samt siden fortsat paa Reisen op igjennem de Forenede Stater i Nordamerica* (reprint, Drammen, Norway: Lyche Grafisk AS, 1995), 9–27; C. A. Clausen, trans. and intro., *A Chronicler of Immigrant Life: Svein Nilsson's Articles in* Billed-Magazin, *1868–1870* (Northfield, MN: NAHA, 1982), 49–66, quotes 50, 51, 54, 56; *Billed-Magazin,* February 20, 1869.

17. Blegen, *Norwegian Migration* (1931), 111, 141, 151, quotes 111, 151; "Report of the Minister of Agriculture of Canada," in the *Sessional Papers of the Parliament of the Province of Canada* 28A (1861); Lovoll, *Promise of America,* 26–28, 53, 58; Qualey, *Norwegian Settlement,* 4–5, 48–49.

NOTES TO CHAPTER 2

1. Nils P. Vigeland, *Norsk seilskipsfart erobrer verdenshavene* (Trondheim, Norway: F. Bruns Bokhandels Forlag, 1943); the reference is to the title of the book. Helge W. Nordvik, "The Shipping Industries of the Scandinavian Countries, 1850–1914," in Lewis R. Fischer and Gerald E. Panting, eds., *Change and Adaptation in Maritime History: The North Atlantic Fleets in the Nineteenth Century* (St. John's: Maritime History Group, Memorial University of Newfoundland, 1985), 119.

2. Henrietta Larson, trans. and ed., "An Immigrant Journey to America in 1854," *Norwegian-American Studies and Records* 3 (1928): 58–61. "The cod was really a fool" is a poor translation of Østerud's pun in Norwegian, "Torsken var riktig en Tosk." Norway Heritage, http://www.norwayheritage.com/p_year.asp?ye=1850, gives information on departures and arrivals of passenger ships 1825–1925 by year, here for 1850.

3. Rolf Danielsen, Ståle Dyrvik, Tore Grønlie, Knut Helle, and Edgar Hovland, *Norway: A History from the Vikings to Our Own Times,* trans. Michael Drake (Oslo: Scandinavian University Press, 1995), 115–16, 123–27, 131, 148–53, 155, 189, 204–5, 206–7, 208–11, 461, 462, quotes 199, 207, 209; Lovoll, *Promise of America,* 1–5; Nils P. Vigeland, *Norsk seilskipsfart,* 69–70. See also Øystein Rian, "Krigenes Norden 1523–1814," and Tore Pryser, "Fra kongemakt til folkemakt," in Henrik S. Nissen, ed., *Nordens historie 1397–1997* (Copenhagen: DR Multimedie, 1997), 39–64, 99–124. Lars Roar Langslet, *Christian Frederik. En biografi* (Oslo: Cappelen Damm, 2014), corrects misconceptions about Christian Frederik and shows that the establishment of an independent Norwegian nation in 1814 was his doing.

4. Gøthe Gøthesen, *Under seil. Sjømannsliv i seilskutetiden* (Oslo: Grøndahl and Søn Forlag A.s., 1982), quote 18; Brit Berggreen, Arne Emil Christensen, and Bård Kolltveit, eds., *Norsk sjøfart* (Oslo: Dreyers Forlag A/S, 1989), 1:27–31; Vigeland, *Norsk seilskipsfart,* 68–70, 74–77, 80, 81, 86.

5. Vigeland, *Norsk seilskipsfart*, 98–99, 100, 101, quotes 87.

6. Scheel and Worm-Müller, *Den norske sjøfarts historie*, 239, 249, 251, quote 235; Bothwell, *Penguin History of Canada*, 196–97, quote 162.

7. Lewis R. Fischer and Even Lange, *Research in Maritime History*, New Directions in Norwegian Maritime History 46 (St. John's, Newfoundland: Maritime Economic History Association, 2011), 14–15; *Morgenbladet*, October 17, 1849; *Drammens Adresse*, June 8, 11, 1850; *Drammens Tidende*, June 7, 1850; Helge W. Nordvik, "Norwegian Emigrants and Canadian Timber: Norwegian Shipping to Quebec, 1850–1875," paper presented at the Meeting of the International Commission for Maritime History, session on "Maritime Aspects of Migration," Comité International des Sciences Historiques Conference, University of Stuttgart, Federal Republic of Germany, August 25–September 1, 1985; report by acting Swedish-Norwegian consul George Pemberton, London, January 31, 1851; Berggreen, Christensen, and Kolltveit, eds., *Norsk sjøfart*, 1:279–80; 1850 report of A. C. Buchanan, chief emigration agent, *Sessional Papers* (1851); Lars Erik Larson, "Norwegian Emigration to Canada 1850–1874," *Chequamegon Bay History* (2010), 4–5; Vigeland, *Norsk seilskipsfart*, quote 215.

8. Blegen, *Norwegian Migration* (1931), 349–51; Julie E. Backer, *Ekteskap, fødsler og vandringer i Norge 1856–1960* (Oslo: Statistisk sentralbyrå, 1965), 158; A. N. Kiær, *Tabeller vedkommende Folkemængdens Bevægelse i Aarene 1856–1865* (Christiania [Oslo]: Departementet for Det Indre, 1868), lxxiii.

9. Kiær, *Tabeller vedkommende Folkemængdens Bevægelse*, lxxiii; A. N. Kiær, *Oversigt over de vigtigste Resultater af de statistiske Tabeller vedkommende Folkemængdens Bevægelse 1866–1885* (Kristiania: Det statistiske Centralbureau, 1890), 110–17; Semmingsen, *Veien mot vest* (1941), 109–10; Blegen, *Norwegian Migration* (1931), 350–51; Nordvik, "Norwegian Emigrants and Canadian Timber," 6, 8; Larson, "Norwegian Emigration to Canada," 6–7; Backer, *Ekteskap, fødsler og vandringer i Norge*, 158–59; Worm-Müller and Scheel, *Den norske sjøfarts historie*, 628–29.

10. Lovoll, *Promise of America*, 13–16, quote 23–24; Backer, *Ekteskap, fødsler og vandringer i Norge*, 158. The dates of the first mass emigration wave are generally given as 1866 to 1873. The emigration in 1874 is here counted in order to include the final direct arrival in Quebec of Norwegian sailing ships with passengers. The number of emigrants in 1873 was 10,352. It dropped to 4,601 in 1874.

11. K. A. Rene, *Historie om udvandringen fra Voss og vossingerne i Amerika* (Madison, WI: Udgivet med støtte af Vosselaget, 1930), 103–12, 132, 179–81, 185; Lovoll, *A Century of Urban Life*, 12, 14–15, 45, 49–50; Semmingsen, *Veien mot vest* (1941), 85; Blegen, *Norwegian Migration* (1931), 86, 136, 360; Eirik Røthe, "The Emigration from Voss to America in

a Nutshell," in *Gamalt frå Voss. Utvandring frå Voss til Amerika. Eit 150-års minne* (Voss, Norway: Voss bygdeboksnemnd, Voss Sogelag, Voss folkemuseum, 1985), 118–135; Odd S. Lovoll, "A Pioneer Chicago Colony from Voss, Norway: Its Impact on Overseas Migration, 1836–60," in Rudolph J. Vecoli and Suzanne M. Sinke, eds., *A Century of European Migrations, 1830–1930* (Chicago: University of Illinois Press, 1991), 182–99. Odd S. Lovoll, "Den tidlige Chicago-kolonien og dens innflytelse på den vestnorske utvandringen," in Ståle Dyrvik and Nils Kolle, eds., *Eit blidare tilvere? Drivkrefeter og motiv i den tidlegaste utvandringa frå Hordaland og Sogn og Fjordane* (Voss, Norway: Voss folkemuseum, 1986), 176–93; George T. Flom, *A History of Norwegian Immigration to the United States from the Earliest Beginning down to the Year 1848* (Iowa City, IA: Privately printed, 1909), 234–35.

The twenty civilian administrative units *amt* (provinces) were on January 1, 1919, replaced with *fylke*, plural *fylker*. The translation "province" is used in the text for *fylke* rather than "county." A *fylke* has a much more complete administrative system than a U.S. county as well as a *fylkesmann*, a district governor, appointed by the Norwegian government. The term *province* consequently becomes a more adequate coinage. The contemporary names of the provinces are employed in this study (see map). They were renamed as follows: 1. Smaalenenes *amt* = Østfold *fylke*, 2. Akershus *amt* = Akershus *fylke*, 3. Kristiania *amt* = Kristiania *fylke*, in 1925 renamed Oslo *fylke*, 4. Hedemarken *amt* = Hedmark *fylke*, 5. Kristians *amt* = Oppland *fylke*, 6. Buskerud *amt* = Buskerud *fylke*, 7. Jarlsberg og Larvik *amt* = Vestfold *fylke*, 8. Bratsberg *amt* = Telemark *fylke*, 9. Nedenes *amt* = Aust-Agder *fylke*, 10. Lister og Mandal *amt* = Vest-Agder *fylke*, 11. Stavanger *amt* = Rogaland *fylke*, 12. Søndre Bergenhus *amt* = Hordaland *fylke*, 13. Bergen *amt* = Bergen *fylke*, 14. Nordre Bergenhus *amt* = Sogn og Fjordane *fylke*, 15. Romsdal *amt* = Møre *fylke*, renamed Møre og Romsdal *fylke* in 1935, 16. Søndre-Trondhjem *amt* = Sør-Trøndelag *fylke*, 17. Nordre-Trondhjem *amt* = Nord-Trøndelag *fylke*, 18. Nordland *amt* = Nordland *fylke*, 19. Tromsø *amt* = Troms *fylke*, 20. Finmarken *amt* = Finmark *fylke*, altered to Finnmark *fylke* in 1925.

The regional names encompassing specific provinces are introduced in the text:

Vestlandet = Rogaland, Hordaland, Sogn og Fjordane, and Møre og Romsdal *fylker*.

Østlandet = generally defined as Østfold, Akershus, Oslo, Hedmark, Oppland, Buskerud, Vestfold, and Telemark *fylker*.

Sørlandet = Vest-Agder and Åust-Agder *fylker* or also in reference to the coastal districts of the two provinces.

12. Blegen, *Norwegian Migration* (1931), 64–70, 353, 360; Semmingsen, *Veien mot vest* (1941), 86. See the discussion of the nature and causes of emigration in Lovoll, *Promise of America*, 13–26; Blegen, *Land of Their Choice*, quote 55; Rasmus Sunde, "Emigration from the District of Sogn, 1839–1915," trans. C. A. Clausen, *Norwegian American Studies* 29 (1983): 111–26, quote 122; Backer, *Ekteskap, fødsler og vandringer i Norge*, 165; "Summariske opgaver over folkemængdens bevægelse m.v. i aarene 1856–1865," in Kiær, *Tabeller vedkommende Folkemængdens Bevægelse*, 4.

13. Leiv H. Dvergdal, "Emigration from Sunnfjord to America prior to 1885," trans. C. A. Clausen, *Norwegian-American Studies* 29 (1983), 127–58; Semmingsen, *Veien mot vest* (1941), 244–45, 246–47; Ingrid Semmingsen, *Veien mot vest. Utvandringen fra Norge 1865–1915* (Oslo: H. Aschehoug & Co. [W. Nygaard], 1950), 2:79, 80–88, quote 79; Lovoll, *Promise of America*, 14–15, 17–18, quote 17; Backer, *Ekteskap, fødsler og vandringer i Norge*, 165; Jostein Molde, "The Emigration from Trøndelag," in *Aarbok 2005. Yearbook of the Trøndelag of America* (Cary, IL: Norskbok Press, 2005), 24–28; Jostein Molde, "Oppbruddet," pages from an unpublished manuscript; Lovoll, "A Pioneer Chicago Colony," 183; Odd S. Lovoll, "Canada Fever: The Odyssey of Minnesota's Bardo Norwegians," *Minnesota History* 57.7 (Fall 2001): 356–67; May Lunde, "Emigration to North America from the Provinces of Troms and Finnmark as Reflected in Three Northern Norwegian Newspapers 1860–1900," in Øyvind T. Gulliksen, Ingeborg R. Kongslien, and Dina Tolfsby, eds., *Essays on Norwegian-American Literature and History* (Oslo: NAHA-Norway, 1990), 2:85–100; May Lunde, "Læstadianske utvandrere fra Nord-Norge til USA,'" in Rolf Svellingen, ed., *Minoritetar frå Noreg til Amerika. Grupper og personar som drog frå Noreg for å oppnå fridom og betre vilkår i USA* (Sletta, Norway: Vestnorsk utvandringssenter, 2007), 33–54; Aarek, "A Short History of the Troms Quakers," 91–140; *Friends Review*, London, 1864, 38; Jacob S. Worm-Müller, "Emigrant- og Kanadafarten," in Scheel and Worm-Müller, eds., *Den norske sjøfarts historie fra de ældste tider til vore dage* (Oslo: Steenske forlag, 1951), 2:601–2; Einar Niemi, "From Northern Scandinavia to the United States: Ethnicity and Migration, the Sami and the Arctic Finns," in Dag Blanck and Per Jegebäck, eds., *Migration och mångfald. Essäer om kulturkontakt och minoritetsfrågor tillägnade Harald Runblom* (Uppsala, Sweden: Centrum för multietnisk forskning, 1999), 155–58, 159–61; "Dissentere i det offentliges arkiver. En presentatsjon av dokumentasjonen på lokalt plan og litt om det den dokumenterer," http://digitalarkivet.no/sab/dissenter.htm.

In his article "The Emigration from Trøndelag," Molde analyzes the unreliable statistics on emigration before 1867 and the official emigration records beginning that year.

14. Semmingsen, *Veien mot vest* (1941), 88–93; Semmingsen, *Veien mot vest* (1950), 2:77; Blegen, *Norwegian Migration* (1931), 358–60; Kiær, *Tabeller vedkommende Folkemængdens Bevægelse* , 178–80; Backer, *Ekteskap, fødsler og vandringer i Norge,* 165; Terje Mikael Hasle Joranger, "Emigration from Reinli, Valdres, to the Upper Midwest: A Comparative Study," *Norwegian-American Studies* 35 (2000): 153–96; Andres A. Svalestuen, "Emigration from the Community of Tinn, 1837–1907: Demographic, Economic, and Social Background," trans. C. A. Clausen, *Norwegian-American Studies* 29 (1983): 43–88; Arnfinn Engen, "Emigration from Dovre, 1865–1914," trans. C. A. Clausen, *Norwegian-American Studies* 29 (1983): 210–52; Hjalmar Rued Holand, *History of the Norwegian Settlements,* trans. Malcolm Rosholt and Helmer M. Blegen, (Decorah, IA: Astri My Astri Publishing, 2006), quote 45; Arne Odd Johnsen, ed., "Johannes Nordboe and Norwegian Immigration: An 'America Letter' of 1837," *Norwegian-American Studies and Records* 8 (1934): 23–38, quote 30.

Laws passed in 1863 and 1869 to control the transportation of passengers and the activities of emigration agents in order to protect people moving to foreign lands improved the reliability of the statistical information. Emigration protocols were kept by the police from 1867.

15. Backer, *Ekteskap, fødsler og vandringer i Norge,* 164, 165; Semmingsen, *Veien mot Vest* (1941), 90–91; Lovoll, *A Century of Urban Life,* 42–43; Molde, "Emigration from Trøndelag," 24–25; Kiær, *Tabeller vedkommende Folkemængdens Bevægelse,* 179, 185–86.

16. Blegen, *Norwegian Migration* (1931), 4–8, quote 159; Eric De Geer, *Migration och influensfält. Studier av emigration och intern migration i Finland och Sverige 1816–1972* (Uppsala, Sweden: Acta Universitas Upsaliensis, 1977); Odd S. Lovoll, "Norwegians on the Land," address for the Society of Local and Regional History, Department of History, Southwest State University, Marshall, MN, 1992; Kiær, *Tabeller vedkommende Folkemængdens Bevægelse,* vii, 175; Semmingsen, *Veien mot vest* (1941), 418–19; Lovoll, *A Century of Urban Life,* 5; Lovoll, *Promise of America,* 19–20; Andres A. Svalestuen, "Professor Ingrid Semmingsen—emigrasjonshistorikeren," in Sivert Langholm and Francis Sejersted, eds., *Vandringer. Festskrift til Ingrid Semmingsen på 70-årsdagen 29. mars 1980* (Oslo: H. Aschehoug and Co. [W. Nygaard], 1980), 9–42; Sima Lieberman, *The Industrialization of Norway, 1800–1920* (Oslo: Universitetsforlaget, 1970), 127–28, quote 127. See Sverre Steen, "Det gamle samfunn," *Det frie Norge,* vol. 4 (Oslo: J. W. Cappelens Forlag, 1957).

17. Jostein Nerbøvik, *Norsk historie 1870–1905* (Oslo: Det norske Samlaget, 1976), 1, 9, 22–24, 40–43, 46, 47–49; Tore Pryser, *Norsk historie 1814–1860. Frå standssamfunn mot klassesamfunn* (Oslo: Det norske Samlaget, 1999), 59–63, 64; Arne Bergsgård, *Norsk*

historie 1814–1880, rev. ed., Dagfinn Mannsåker and Magne Skodvin (Oslo: Det norske Samlaget, 1964), 114–16, 117–21, 126, quote 126; Danielsen, et al., *Norway*, 260–61; Lovoll, *Promise of America*, 22–26, 58–59; Backer, *Ekteskap, fødsler og vandringer i Norge*, 166, 167. See also Magnus Nodtvedt, *Rebirth of Norway's Peasantry: Folk Leader Hans Nielsen Hauge* (Tacoma, WA: Pacific Lutheran University Press, 1965).

18. Berggreen, Christensen, and Kolltveit, eds., *Norsk sjøfart*, 2:67–68, 71; Vigeland, *Norsk seilskipsfart*, quote 93; Gøthesen, *Under seil*, 7, 22, 26, 30–31, 33–36, 40, 42–43, 52–53, quote 33; Lauritz Pettersen, *Bergen og sjøfarten. Fra kjøpmannsrederi til selvstendig næring 1860–1914* (Bergen, Norway: Bergens rederiforening og Bergens sjøfartsmuseum, 1981), 3:82–83.

One metric ton equals 1,016 kilograms or 2,240 pounds.

19. Vigeland, *Norsk seilskipsfart*, 130–31, 137–38, 167–209, 253–61; Gøthesen, *Under seil*, 13; Semmingsen, *Veien mot vest* (1941), 91–92, 244–45, 416; Semmingsen, *Veien mot vest* (1950), 2:221; Lovoll, *Promise of America*, 17–18; Johs B. Thue, *Bergen og sjøfarten. Skipsfart og kjøpmannsskap 1800–1860* (Bergen, Norway: Bergens rederiforening, 1980), 2:81–107; Pettersen, *Bergen og sjøfarten*, 3:38–45, 68–69, 71–72; Berggreen, Christensen, and Kolltveit, eds., *Norsk sjøfart*, 2:48–50; Berggreen, Christensen, and Kolltveit, eds., *Norsk sjøfart*, 1:268–69; Odd Magnar Syversen and Derwood Johnson, *Norge i Texas. Et bidrag til norsk migrasjonshistorie* (Stange, Norway: Stange historielag, 1982), 23–55; Nordvik, "Shipping Industries of the Scandinavian Countries," 131–32, quote 132; Sverre Ordahl, "Emigration from Agder to America, 1890–1915," trans. C. A. Clausen, *Norwegian-American Studies* 29 (1983), 313–38. See Johan Reinert Reiersen, *Pathfinder for Norwegian Emigrants*, trans. Frank G. Nelson (Northfield, MN: NAHA, 1981).

NOTES TO CHAPTER 3

1. Kiær, *Tabeller vedkommende Folkemængdens Bevægelse*, lxxiii, 179–60, 191–92; Vigeland, *Norsk seilskipsfart*, 115; "Ombord i et Emigrantskib," in *Skilling-Magazin. Til Udbredelse af Almennyttige Kundskaber*, March 21, 1868; Lovoll, *Promise of America*, 28; *Christiania-Posten*, February 5, 1853; Semmingsen, *Veien mot vest* (1950), 2:86–87, quote 87; Blegen, *Norwegian Migration* (1931), 136–37; Pettersen, *Bergen og sjøfarten*, 3:50, 55.

2. Odd S. Lovoll, "En utvandringsagent på Ringsaker," *Heimen* 3 (1979): xviii, 149–56; Kristian Hvidt, "Emigration Agents: The Development of a Business and Its Methods," *Scandinavian Journal of History* 3 (1978): 179–203; *Morgenbladet*, December 21, 1866; Allan Line newspaper advertisement; *Stavanger Amtstidende*, April 15, 1861; *Throndhjems borgerlige Realskoles alene privilegerendeAdressecontors-Efterretninger*, March 9, 1862; Lovoll, *Promise of America*, 25, 30; Niemi, "From Northern Scandinavia to the United

States," 164. Odd S. Lovoll, *Norwegian Newspapers in America: Connecting Norway and the New Land* (St. Paul: Minnesota Historical Society Press, 2010), 27–29, 34–35, 39–40; *Christiania-Posten*, February 17, March 17, 31, April 15, 1853; *Morgenbladet*, May 14, 1850, February 6, 14, 1853; *Stavanger Amtstidende*, February 22, March 1, 1851, April 5, 1853; *Emigranten*, April 16, December 26, 1852, March 17, 25, July 1, 27, 29, August 5, 12, 19, 1853, February 16, April 27, October 12, 1855, December 22, 1858; Semmingsen, *Veien mot vest* (1941), 148–50; Blegen, *Norwegian Migration* (1931), 339–42; information on Helge Haugan from the Drammen Public Library.

Scholars disagree on the influence emigration agents had on people's decision to emigrate. Semmingsen, *Veien mot vest* (1950), 2:86–139, is the most comprehensive treatment of Norwegian emigration agents, and their significance is emphasized. Danish scholar Kristian Hvidt, in "Emigration Agents" and other publications, agrees with Semmingsen in his own findings regarding Danish emigration agents. Swedish scholars Berit Brattne, *Bröderna Larsson. En studie i svensk emigrantagentverksamhet under 1880-talet* (Uppsala, Sweden: Studia Historica Upsaliensia, 1973), and Hans Norman, *Från Bergslagen till Nordamerika. Studier i migrationsmönster, social rörlighet och demografisk strukturmed utgångspunkt från Örebro län 1851–1915* (Uppsala, Sweden: Studia Historica Upsaliensia, 1974), both disagree, concluding that the emigration agents' influence on the stream of emigrants was minimal, as the spread of information about America already was a fact. Later in the nineteenth century, travel bureaus replaced the system of agents.

3. Oliver Mac Donagh, *A Pattern of Government Growth, 1800–1860* (London: Mac Gibbon and Kee, 1961), 202n52; "Dictionary of Canadian Biography Online"; *Sessional Papers* (1861); Larson, "Norwegian Emigration to Canada," 23; Theodore C. Blegen, *The Norwegian Migration to America* (Northfield, MN: NAHA, 1940), 2:363, 368; Orm Øverland, "Håpefulle utvandrere og en utro tjener" in *Ætt og Heim* (Stavanger, Norway: Rogaland historielag, 1994), 130–31, 132; Per Fuglum, *Asbjørn Kloster. Pedagog, forkynner og avholdspioner* (Oslo: Lunde forlag, 2004), 362; circular dated August 1859 in Archives of the Society of Friends, in the State Archives in Stavanger; letter from Closter to Asbjørn Kloster dated in 1859, in Archives of the Society of Friends; Anton Jorgensen, "Foreign Immigration, December 14, 1864," in *Sessional Papers* (1865). Blegen has changed Haugan to Haugen, though the former is according to sources the correct form.

4. Emigration (North America), British Parliamentary Papers, Colonies, Canada, vol. 19 (1850–51), 422, 476; Vigeland, *Norsk seilskipsfart*, 113–14; Berggreen, Christensen, and Kolltveit, eds., *Norsk sjøfart*, 1:302; Worm-Müller and Scheel, *Den norske sjøfartshistorie*, 2:595, 602–3, 604–6, 620, 623–24, 625–26, quote 624; Theodore C.

Blegen, trans. and ed., *Ole Rynning's True Account of America* (Northfield, MN: NAHA, 1926), 99; Liv Marit Haakenstad, *Slektsgranskerens guide til utvandringen 1825–1930* (Oslo: Orion Forlag AS, 2008), 46–49; Clara Jacobson, "En Amerika-reise for seksti aar siden," in Kristian Prestgard and Johs. B. Wist, eds., *Symra. Et skrift for norske paa begge sider av havet* (Decorah, IA: The Symra Company, 1913), 120, 125.

5. Nordvik, "Norwegian Emigrants and Canadian Timber," 8, 11, 12–13; Larson, "Norwegian Emigration to Canada," 7; Worm-Müller and Scheel, *Den norske sjøfarts-historie*, 2:566, 611, quote 611; Vigeland, *Norsk seilskipsfart*, 215; *Folkemængdensbevægelse, 1866–1885*, 115–17.

6. Larson, "Norwegian Emigration to Canada," 6–7; Nordvik, "Norwegian Emigrants and Canadian Timber," 11; Semmingsen, *Veien mot vest* (1941), 110; Edwin C. Guillet, *The Great Migration: The Atlantic Crossing by Sailing-ship Since 1770* (New York: Thomas Nelson and Sons, 1937), 233–48; Worm-Müller and Scheel, *Den norske sjø-fartshistorie*, 2:627–28; Berggreen, Christensen, and Kolltveit, eds., *Norsk sjøfart*, 2:147–50; Royal Swedish and Norwegian Consulate, reports dated January 26, 1863, February 8, 1866, January 15, 29, 1867, January 20, 1873, in the National Archives in Oslo; *Uddrag af Consulatberetninger vedkommende Norges Handel og Skibsfart i Aaret 1871* (Christiania, Norway: Departementet for Det Indre, 1872), 60, 71, 72, 73–74, 86; *Tabeller vedkommende Folkemængdens Bevægelse i Aaret 1866* (Christiania, Norway: Departementet for Det Indre, 1869), xv–xvi, xviii; *Tabeller vedkommende Folkemængdens Bevægelse i Aaret 1869* (Christiania, Norway: Departementet for Det Indre, 1872), xiv. See the overview given by Børge Solem, "With the Biggest and Fastest Ships . . . ," trans. Harry T. Cleven (Oslo: Norskamerikanske avdeling–Nasjonalbiblioteket, 2000), 8.

7. Norway Heritage, http://www.norwayheritage.com/p_shiplist.asp, has been consulted in regard to the Wilson Line; Qualey, *Norwegian Settlement*, 251; Worm-Müller and Scheel, *Den norske sjøfartshistorie*, 2:628; Semmingsen, *Veien mot vest* (1950), 2:162–65; Odd S. Lovoll, "'For People Who Are Not in a Hurry': The Danish Thingvalla Line and the Transportation of Scandinavian Emigrants," *Journal of American Ethnic History* 13.1 (Fall 1993): 48–67; Lovoll, *Promise of America*, 28–29.

8. Worm-Müller and Scheel, *Den norske sjøfartshistorie*, 2:613, 614, 620, quote 514; "Med Arendals-barken Valkyrien over havet," article in collection of Bergens sjø-fartsmuseum; C. K. Fjærestad, "The Emigrant Ship *Valkyrien*," in Marget Nysetvold Bakke, ed., *Norwegians in America, Their History and Record*, trans. Olaf Tronsen Kringhaug and Odd-Steinar Dybvad Raneng (Waukon, IA: Astri My Astri Publishing, 2010), 1:205–14. The bark *Valkyrien* was a well-constructed ship and continued to transport cargo for another thirty-four years.

9. Marianna O'Gallagher, *Grosse Ile: Gateway to Canada, 1832–1937* (Ste. Foy, Québec: Carraig Books, 1984), 15, 25–26, 38, 43, 47–58, 70–71, 88, quote 52; Jeannette Vekeman Masson, *A Grandmother Remembers Grosse Ile,* trans. Johanne L. Massé (Ste. Foy, Québec: Carraig Books, 1989), 167–78: Jorgensen, *Emigration from Europe,* 7–8; Andrew Andersen, letter dated April 20, 1868; Frederick Montizambert, M.D., letter dated November 28, 1866; Andrew Andersen, letter dated November 29, 1866, all in Bureau of Agriculture, Emigration and Statistics Library and Archives Canada, Ottawa, ON; Worm-Müller and Scheel, *Den norske sjøfartshistorie,* 2:621–22, quote 621; A. C. Buchanan, "Emigration Report," *Sessional Papers* 16.7 (1858); Larson, "Norwegian Emigration to Canada," 21, 29; André Charbonneau and André Sevigny, Statistics on Immigration and Quarantine. The Quarantine Station on Grosse Ile, 1832–1937; National Historic Site of Canada, Grosse Ile and the Memorial of Irish, list of names of the memorial, 1832–1934, available: http://www.pc.gc.ca/lhn-nhs/qc/grosseile/natcul/natcul4_E.asp; notes from author's visit to Grosse Île, September 15, 2012; "Extracts from the Immigration Report of 1862," taken from the Immigration Report in the British Parliamentary Papers 1863, 15.3 (1991): 247.

The parliamentary report's percentage of Norwegian deaths is based on a lower number of emigrants than published in Norwegian statistics, but in comparison to German deaths among the 2,516 German emigrants listed in the report, the number of Norwegian emigrants who perished is indeed a disturbing figure.

10. *Tabeller vedrørende Folkemængdens Bevægelse,* 1869, xvi; Backer, *Ekteskap, fødsler og vandringer i Norge,* 171, 173; Larson, "Norwegian Emigration to Canada," 8; Gustaf Elgenstierna, *Den introducerade svenska adelns ättartavlor,* 1925–36, available: http://www .adelsvapen.com/genealogi/Falkenberg_af_Trystorp_nr_255, tab 33; Semmingsen, *Veien mot vest* (1950), 2:50; L. Stafford to J. C. Lachie, telegraph, July 11, 1868, Bureau of Agriculture, Emigration and Statistics, Library and Archives Canada, Ottawa, ON; Immigrant Ships Transcribers Guild, http://immigrantships.net/1800/ann adelius670601.html. Anticosti Island is located at the outlet of the St. Lawrence River into the Gulf of St. Lawrence.

11. A. C. Buchanan, "Nine and Twentieth Annual Report of the Chief Agent of Immigration 1866," *Sessional Papers* 3A (1867); see also Larson, "Norwegian Emigration to Canada," 29–30; *Emigranten,* February 2, 1855; Annual Report of the Emigration Agent at Quebec for 1868, *Sessional Papers* 76A (1869); *Uddrag af Consulatberetninger vedkommende Norges Handel og Skibsfart i Aaret 1871,* 72; report of "A Special Meeting of the Emigrants' Society held in the Court-house at Quebec, the 11th October, 1819," courthouse, Quebec City; *Quebec Emigrant Society. Proceedings of a Special Public Meeting*

April 28, 1832 (Quebec: T. Cary and Co., 1832); O'Gallagher, *Grosse Ile,* 18, 49, 54, quote 18; Internet search on Montreal Emigrant Society; Report of the Select Committee to Whom Was Referred the Annual Report of the Chief Emigration Agent, in *Sessional Papers* 21 (1860); Return, *Sessional Papers,* 18.3 (1860). See also Robert Vineberg, *Responding to Immigrants' Settlement Needs: The Canadian Experience* (New York: SpringerBriefs in Population Studies, 2011).

12. Paul W. Gates, "Official Encouragement to Immigration by the Province of Canada," *The Canadian Historical Review* 15 (1934): 24–38; Mauri A. Jalava, "The Scandinavians as a Source of Settlers for the Dominion of Canada: The First Generation," *Scandinavian-Canadian Studies* (1983): 3–14; A. C. Buchanan, Emigration Report, 1856, *Sessional Papers* 47A (1857); Larson, "Norwegian Emigration to Canada," 11.

13. *Uddrag af Connsulatberetninger 1871,* 74; Judith Fingard, *Jack in Port: Sailortowns of Eastern Canada* (Toronto: University of Toronto Press, 1982), 3, 5, 18–19, 49–50, 186, 197–98; correspondence with Professor Judith Fingard, Dalhousie University, Halifax; Johan Nicolay Tønnesen, "Rømning 1850–1914 fra norske skip i fremmede havner," in *Den norske sjøfarts historie fra de ældste tider til vore dage* (Oslo: J. W. Cappelens forlag, 1951), 2:148–66, quote 150; Catharina B. Dyvik, "Hiding Migrants: A Study of Seamen Deserting from Norwegian Merchant Vessels between 1860 and 1914," MSe economic history, London School of Economics, 2011, 4–8; Wilhelm Anthony Schwartz, Consulatberetningerfor 1871, *Uddrag af Consulatberetninger 1871;* Helge W. Nordvik, "A Crucial Six Percent Norwegian Sailors in the Canadian Merchant Marine, 1863–1913," in *Sjøfartshistorisk årbok 1984* (Bergen, Norway: Foreningen-Bergens sjøfartsmuseum, 1985), 139–59; Worm-Müller and Scheel, *Den norske sjøfartshistorie,* 2:579–83; Berggreen, Christensen, and Kolltveit, eds., *Norsk sjøfart,* 2:113–14.

14. L. S. Channell, comp., *History of Compton County and Sketches of the Eastern Townships, District of St. Francis, and Sherbrooke County* (Cookshire, Quebec: L. S. Channell, 1896), 7–8, 242–43; Glen Brown, "The British American Land Company: Reading Given to the Stanstad Historical Society, August 2nd, 1969, at Stanstad Plain," in collection of La Société d'Histoirie de Sherbrooke, Sherbrooke, Quebec; Jean-Pierre Kesteman, *Histoirie de Sherbrooke, 1802–1866* (Sherbrooke, Quebec: G. G. C., 2000), 1:114, 153; Emigration Report, 1854, Parliament House of Commons Session 1854–55, 39.13; Martin Ulvestad, "De förste norske Settlementer i Canada," in *Norsk-Amerikaneren* (Seattle, WA: Martin Ulvestad, 1823), 249–50; Christopher O. Closter, letter, in annual report, *Sessional Papers* 19A (1859); Christopher O. Closter, letter, in annual report, *Sessional Papers* 18A (1860); Christopher O. Closter, letter, in annual report, *Sessional Papers* 14A (1861); Harold Owen Peter Engen, "A History of the

Evangelical Lutheran Church in Canada," Bachelor of Divinity Degree, Luther Theological Seminary, Saskatoon, 1955, 8; *Le Pionnier,* August 28, 1868, trans. Estelle Bourbeau and Chloé Ouellet-Riendeau, La Société d'histoire de Sherbrooke, Sherbrooke, Quebec; Johan Schrøder, *Skandinaverne i De forenede Stater og Canada* (reprint, La Crosse, WI: Trygt og forlagt af Forfatteren, 1867), 45, 53; James Knutson, Waterville, Quebec, provided information on the 1901 regional census. See also Orm Øverland, trans. and intro., *Johan Schrøder's Travels in Canada 1863* (Montreal: McGill-Queen's University Press, 1989).

15. Annual Report, *Sessional Papers* (1860); Fabien Sinnett and Martin Mimeault, *Gaspé au fil du temps,* trans. Mary Cisar (Gaspé, Quebec: Musée de la Gaspésie, 2009), 184; Martin Mimeault, *Le Porte Franc de'Gaspé,* trans. Mary Cisar (Gaspé, Quebec: Musée de la Gaspésie, 1998), 39; Blegen, *Norwegian Migration* (1940), 367; Jean-Marie Fallu, *Une histoire d'appartenance,* trans. Mary Cisar, *La Gaspesie,* 7:250, states a payment period of land at five years while Blegen has twenty years.

The Canadian government also tried in the mid-1850s to create a settlement for Norwegians in the Ottawa country, south of the Ottawa River, westward from Ottawa City to Lake Huron. In the emigration report for 1863, A. C. Buchanan claims that the German settlements were progressing favorably while the Norwegians "are abandoning this part of the Province altogether."

16. Closter's letter and Buchanan's report, in annual report, *Sessional Papers* (1860); information on family history provided by Susie Ruchie, Donna, and John Haines; Semmingsen, *Veien mot vest* (1950), 2:98; Helge Haugan, letter, *Sessional Papers* (1861); *Stavanger Amtstidende og Adresseavis,* December 9, 1861; Blegen, *Norwegian Migration* (1940), 370; N. C. Brun, "Første aars oplevelser," *Symra. En aarbog for norske paa begge sider af havet* 7.2 (1911): 110–19.

17. *Stavanger Amtstidende og Adresseavis,* January 7, 10, March 20, 27, April 4, 8, 15, 1861, April 7, 1862; Ken Annett, "Gaspé of Yesterday: The Saga of the High Hopes and Brave Attempt to Found a Norwegian Colony in Gaspé and of the Colony's Fate," copy in author's possession; Blegen, *Norwegian Migration* (1940), 374; Ommer, *From Outpost to Outport;* Doug Ford, *Chasing the Cod: Jerseymen in Canada* (Jersey: Jersey Heritage Trust, 2007); Report of the Commissioner of Crown Lands of Canada, *Sessional Papers* 3 (1862); Øverland, "Håpefulle utvandrere," 133–37; Orm Øverland, "The Norwegian Settlement in Gaspé, 1860–1862: The Failure of the Canadian Bureau of Agriculture or of the Land?" *Norse Heritage* (Stavanger, Norway: The Norwegian Emigration Center, 1991), 2:72–81; Brun, "Første aars oplevelser," 238. Professor Jean-Marie Thibeault provided information on Thomas Le Page and Bougainville.

18. Carl Schölström to Asbjørn Kloster, March 1, May 20, 22, 1861, March 15, 1862, January 8, 1867, in Archives of the Society of Friends, State Archives, Stavanger; Blegen, *Norwegian Migration* (1940), 371, 375, 377; Annett, "Gaspé of Yesterday"; Brun, "Første aars oplevelser," 116–17; *The Globe,* February 15, 1869; Øverland, "Håpefulle utvandrere," 140–41; Øverland, "The Norwegian Settlement," 80–81; Clara Jacobson, "Days That Are Gone," in Charlotte Jacobson, comp., *Pioneer Memoirs of the Jacobson Immigration and Pioneer Life* (Northfield, MN: NAHA, 1975); Annual Report of the Minister of Agriculture and Statistics for the Year 1862, *Sessional Papers* 4A (1863); Schrøder, *Skandinaverne,* 77.

19. Gary Caldwell, *Histoire de Waterville/History of Waterville* (Sherbrooke: Bibliothèque Nationale du Quebec, 2001), 8–10, 12–18, 25–26; Donald Knutson, *The Knutson Family History* (privately published), 198–206; Ragnar Standal, *Mot nye heimland. Utvandringa frå Hjørundfjord, Vartdal og Ørsta* (Volda, Norway: Utvandrarnemnda, Bygdeboknemndene, Ørsta kommune, 1985), 334–39; James Knutson, "Swedeville, A Few Memories," copy in author's possession; Report of the Minister of Agriculture, *Sessional Papers* 6A (1880); James Knutson, mail to author, August 16, 2014.

NOTES TO CHAPTER 4

1. Johan Fredrik Bockelie, "Utvandrede Bockelie slekten" and "Diary of Martinius Andreas Normann." Bockelie received the diary in 1989. His great-grandfather Ole Bockelie was a passenger on the *Bergen.*

2. Halle Steensland, "Erindringer fra min Amerika-reise og mine første aar i Amerika," *Symra* 5 (1909): 80–89, quotes 85, 86; Emigration, British Parliamentary Papers, Colonies, Canada, vol. 19 (1850–51); Papers relative to Emigration to the North American Colonies, British Parliamentary Papers, Colonies, Canada, vol. 20 (1852–54); Knut Gjerset, *Norwegian Sailors on the Great Lakes* (Northfield, MN: NAHA, 1928), 5–7, 75, 106–7; Henrietta Larson, "The Sinking of the *Atlantic* on Lake Erie," *Norwegian-American Studies and Records* 4 (1929): 92–98; George Pemberton, acting consul of Sweden and Norway, Quebec, letter to the Royal Norwegian Government, December 21, 1852; *Morgenbladet,* June 8, 1852.

3. Joy Sundrum of Golden Valley, Minnesota, provided the Rye biography and other material on her family history.

4. *Chicago Tribune,* August 2, 1862; Lovoll, *A Century of Urban Life,* 72–73, 74–77; Lovoll, *Norwegian Newspapers in America,* 1, 3; *Skandinaven,* June 1, July 26, 1866, August 29, 1867; Odd S. Lovoll, "A Perspective on the Life of Norwegian America: Norwegian Enclaves in Chicago in the 1920s," in Anne Birgit Larsen and Reidar Bakken,

eds., *Migranten/The Migrant* 1 (1988): 26–30; A. E. Strand, *A History of the Norwegians in Illinois* (Chicago: John Anderson Publishing Co., 1905), 342–43; *Morgenavisen*, March 29, 1963; *Nationen*, March 18, 1963.

5. Theodore C. Blegen, "An Early Settlement in Canada," *Rapports annuels de la Société Historique du Canada* 9.1 (1930): quote 88; *Emigranten*, December 8, 1854; Gates, "Official Encouragement to Immigration," 24–38, quote 37.

6. Paul W. Gates, "The Campaign of the Illinois Central Railroad for Norwegian and Swedish Immigrants," *Norwegian-American Studies and Records* 6 (1931): 66–88, quote 88; Theodore C. Blegen, "The Competition of the Northwestern States for Immigrants," *Wisconsin Magazine of History* 3.1 (September 1919): 3–29; Qualey, *Norwegian Settlement*, 36–37.

The Swedish Augustana College in Paxton had begun as a seminary in Chicago in 1860. Since 1872 it has been located in Rock Island, Illinois, as the Augustana College and Theological Seminary.

7. Lovoll, *A Century of Urban Life*, 37; *Daily Democrat*, October 12, November 21, 1848; Blegen, "The Competition of the Northwestern States," 15, 16–17, 18–19.

8. Qualey, *Norwegian Settlement*, 40, 70, 73–74; Donna Haines, "Høynes to America," a family history in author's possession; information on the Brandt family and related topics from Susan Ruchie; Schrøder, *Skandinaverne*, 190–220, traces Norwegian settlement in great detail; Lovoll, *Promise of America*, 64–68; information on "The Theiges Emigrate" from Jean Theige Marck.

9. Livia Apppel and Theodore C. Blegen, "Official Encouragement of Immigration to Minnesota during the Territorial Period," *Minnesota History Bulletin* 5.3 (August 1923): 167–71, quote 195–96; Theodore C. Blegen, "Minnesota's Campaign for Immigrants," *Yearbook of Swedish Historical Society of America* 11 (1926): 3–36; Lars Ljungmark, *For Sale—Minnesota: Organized Promotion of Scandinavian Immigration, 1866–1873* (Stockholm: Akademiförlaget, 1971), 17–18, 19–20, 42–43, 57–61, 65, 78, 121, 130; Qualey, *Norwegian Settlement*, 70, 97–98, 100–101, 109, 112, 128; Lovoll, *Promise of America*, 115; Blegen, *Norwegian Migration* (1931), 343–44; Odd S. Lovoll, *Norwegians on the Prairie: Ethnicity and the Development of the Country Town* (St. Paul: Minnesota Historical Society Press, 2006), 39–40; *Nordisk Folkeblad*, July 31, 1869; Lovoll, *Norwegian Newspapers in America*, 99–100.

10. Marcus Lee Hansen, "Official Encouragement of Immigration to Iowa," *Iowa Journal of History and Politics* 19.2 (April 1921): 159–195; Odd Magnar Syversen and Derwood Johnson, *Norge i Texas. Et bidrag til norsk emigrasjonshistorie* (Stange, Norway: Stange historielag, 1982), 63–73, 107–25, 304; Qualey, *Norwegian Settlement*, 81, 85, 88,

91–92, 227, 228, quote 91–92; Flom, *Norwegian Immigration*, 363, 368–70; Blegen, *Norwegian Migration* (1931), 36–66; *Emigranten*, July 1, 1853; Lovoll, *Promise of America*, 116–17.

11. Qualey, *Norwegian Settlement*, 133–34, 238, 240; Lovoll, *Promise of America*, 122–26; Gordon L. Iseminger, *"Land and Emigration:* A Northern Pacific Railroad Company Newspaper," *North Dakota Quarterly* (Summer 1981): 70–71, 76. James N. Berdahl generously provided the autobiography by Erick J. Berdahl and other information about his family, which includes the author Ole E. Rølvaag and Jeannie Marie Berdahl, whom Rølvaag married in 1908.

NOTE TO EPILOGUE

1. Statistics Canada, 2011 National Household Survey, Tabulation: Ethnic Origin, Single and Multiple Ethnic Origin Responses; Backer, *Ekteskap, fødsler og vandringer i Norge,* 159; Lovoll, "Canada Fever," 56–67; Kenneth O. Bjork, "Scandinavian Migration to the Canadian Prairie Provinces, 1893–1914," *Norwegian-American Studies* 26 (1974): 3–30; Joan Magee, *A Scandinavian Heritage* (Toronto: Dundurn Press Limited, 1985), 27–41; Joh. G. Sandsmark, *Til Amerika og Canada. Canadian Pacific Linjen* (Stavanger, Norway: Joh. G. Sandsmark, 1908), 3–8.

Index

Page numbers in *italics* refer to illustrations